Originally published in German as Number VI of the
"Studien der Bibliothek Warburg," under the
editorship of Fritz Saxl.

LANGUAGE and MYTH

By ERNST CASSIRER

LATE VISITING PROFESSOR OF PHILOSOPHY
COLUMBIA UNIVERSITY

TRANSLATED BY

SUSANNE K. LANGER

AUTHOR OF
Philosophy in a New Key

DOVER PUBLICATIONS INC.
NEW YORK

Standard Book Number: 486-20051-5
Library of Congress Catalog Card Number: 53-9352

Manufactured in the United States of America
Dover Publications, Inc.
180 Varick Street
New York, N. Y. 10014

Dedicated to my Father-in-Law,

OTTO BONDY,

upon the occasion of his

eightieth birthday.

E. C.

TRANSLATOR'S PREFACE

TWENTY-TWO years ago, Ernst Cassirer published the first volume of a work which struck a new note in so-called "theory of knowledge." It was called *Die Philosophie der Symbolischen Formen* (*The Philosophy of Symbolic Forms*). In this work, the "theory of knowledge" became a theory of *mental activity*, which gave as minute and scholarly attention to the forms of feeling and imagination as to the categories of sense perception and logic.

The book has not yet been translated into English; the only access we have to his ideas, therefore, is his recent small volume, *An Essay on Man*, which presents his main conclusions in brief résumé. But to be presented with a thinker's conclusions, not really seeing the path whereby he reached them, or knowing the first suggestion—the insight or naïve perception—which opened that path, is unsatisfactory to anyone whose philosophical interest is more than skin deep.

Now fortunately, at the time when Professor Cassirer was engrossed in the first half of his great work—tracing the story of human mentality *before* the birth of that rather abstract form of conception which we call "logic" —he wrote a short but faithful account of his growing idea, his theory of myth and language. This little study, entitled *Sprache und Mythos*, reveals the genesis of some of those great conclusions for which he is known to the world; it gives one a look into the mental laboratory where new ideas are generated and developed.

Americans like to look into laboratories, especially when they know that something big is in the making there. So this philosophical fragment which prepares a whole world view is here presented to the English-speaking public, for the same reason that the Bibliothek Warburg (one of the world's great ventures in popular education) saw fit to publish it originally.

But an expert in his sanctum sometimes appears to make strange moves, unless we know what he is trying to do. A layman seriously watching him may well appreciate a tip to that effect from some fellow worker in the place. Therefore I may be permitted to point out in advance what Professor Cassirer was undertaking, and how he proposed to do it.

He was originally struck with the fact that the "theory of knowledge," as philosophers had developed it since the Middle Ages, concerned itself solely with the appreciation of "facts" and the development of orderly thought about facts. The inveterate belief of all mankind in myth, sometimes crystallized into dogmas, sometimes degraded into vulgar superstition, was always excluded from the field of philosophical interest, either as divine revelation, which philosophy could not touch, or (especially in modern times) as a miscarriage of logical explanation, a product of ignorance. But the whole realm of mythical concepts is too great a phenomenon to be accounted for as a "mistake" due to the absence of logically recorded facts. Mere ignorance should be agnostic—empty and negative—not exciting and irrepressible. And it dawned on the philosopher that *theory of mind* might well begin not with the analysis of knowledge, but with a search for the reason and spiritual function of this peculiar sort of "ignorance."

Here he was helped by a stroke of insight: the realization that *language*, man's prime instrument of reason, reflects his mythmaking tendency more than his rationalizing tendency. Language, the symbolization of thought, exhibits two entirely different *modes* of thought. Yet in both modes the mind is powerful and creative. It expresses itself in different forms, one of which is discursive logic, the other creative imagination.

Human intelligence begins with *conception*, the prime mental activity; the process of conception always culminates in *symbolic expression*. A conception is fixed and held only when it has been embodied in a symbol. So the study of symbolic forms offers a key to the forms of human conception. The genesis of symbolic forms— verbal, religious, artistic, mathematical, or whatever modes of expression there be—is the odyssey of the mind.

The two oldest of these modes seem to be language and myth. Since both are of prehistoric birth, we cannot fix the age of either; but there are many reasons for regarding them as twin creatures. The intuitions about nature and man reflected in the oldest verbal roots, and the processes by which language probably grew up are the same elementary intuitions and the same processes which are expressed in the development of myths. They are not the categories and canons of so-called "discursive logic," the forms of reason, which underlie both common sense and science. Reason is not man's primitive endowment, but his *achievement*. The seeds of it—fertile, yet long dormant—lie in language; logic springs from language when that greatest of symbolic modes is mature (as it is by the time we meet it in history or ethnology).

Myth never breaks out of the magic circle of its figurative ideas. It reaches religious and poetic heights; but the gulf between its conceptions and those of science never narrows the least bit. But language, born in that same magic circle, has the power to break its bounds; language takes us from the mythmaking phase of human mentality to the phase of logical thought and the conception of facts.

Theory of knowledge has always treated this final achievement as man's natural and primitive way of thinking, and taken "facts" as his earliest stock in trade. Consequently, it could find no connection at all between myth and truth, poetry and common sense, religion and science; most of man's actual ideas, most of his cultural and spiritual background, had to be discounted as error, caprice, or emotional indulgence. Professor Cassirer's great thesis, based on the evidence of language and verified by his sources with quite thrilling success, is that *philosophy of mind involves much more than a theory of knowledge; it involves a theory of prelogical conception and expression, and their final culmination in reason and factual knowledge.*

Such a view changes our whole picture of human mentality. The following pages give the reader the high lights of significant fact which suggested, supported, and finally clinched the theory. I offer the translation of this little study (with some slight modifications and abridgments made by the author shortly before his death) both as a statement of a new philosophical insight and as a revelation of the philosopher's work: his material, his technique, and the solution of the problem by a final flash of interpretive genius.

S. K. L.

New York City
November 1, 1945

CONTENTS

LANGUAGE AND MYTH

The Place of Language
and Myth in the Pattern of
Human Culture

THE opening passage of the Platonic dialogue *Phaedrus*
describes how Socrates lets Phaedrus, whom he encoun-
ters, lure him beyond the gates of the city to the banks
of Ilissus. Plato has pictured the setting of this scene in
nicest detail, and there lies over it a glamour and fra-
grance well-nigh unequaled in classical descriptions of
nature. In the shade of a tall plane tree, at the brink of
a cool spring, Socrates and Phaedrus lie down; the sum-
mer breeze is mild and sweet and full of the cicada's
song. In the midst of this landscape Phaedrus raises the
question whether this be not the place where, according
to a myth, Boreas carried off the fair Orithyia; for the
water is clear and translucent here, fitting for maidens to
sport in and bathe. Socrates, when pressed with ques-
tions as to whether he believes this tale, this "mythol-
ogemen," replies that, although he cannot be said to be-
lieve it, yet he is not at a loss as to its significance. "For,"
he says, "then I could proceed as do the learned, and say
by way of clever interpretation, that Orithyia, while play-
ing with her companion Pharmacia, had been borne over
yonder cliffs by Boreas the Northwind, and because of

this manner of her death she was said to have been carried off by the god Boreas. . . . But I," he adds, "for my part, Phaedrus, I find that sort of thing pretty enough, yet consider such interpretations rather an artificial and tedious business, and do not envy him who indulges in it. For he will necessarily have to account for centaurs and the chimaera, too, and will find himself overwhelmed by a very multitude of such creatures, gorgons and pegasuses and countless other strange monsters. And whoever discredits all these wonderful beings and tackles them with the intention of reducing them each to some probability, will have to devote a great deal of time to this bootless sort of wisdom. But I have no leisure at all for such pastimes, and the reason, my dear friend, is that as yet I cannot, as the Delphic precept has it, know myself. So it seems absurd to me that, as long as I am in ignorance of myself, I should concern myself about extraneous matters. Therefore I let all such things be as they may, and think not of them, but of myself—whether I be, indeed, a creature more complex and monstrous than Typhon, or whether perchance I be a gentler and simpler animal, whose nature contains a divine and noble essence." (*Phaedrus*, 229D ff.)

This sort of myth interpretation, which the Sophists and Rhetoricians of the time held in high repute as the flower of polite learning and the height of the urbane spirit, seemed to Plato the very opposite of this spirit; but although he denounced it as such, calling it a rustic science (ἄγροικος σοφία), his judgment did not prevent the learned from indulging in this sort of wisdom for centuries to come. As the Sophists and Rhetoricians vied with each other at this intellectual sport in Plato's day, so the Stoics and Neoplatonists did in the Hellenistic period. And it was ever and always the science of language, of etymology, that served as a vehicle for such research. Here in the realm of spooks and daemons, as well as in the higher reaches of mythology, the Faustian word seemed ever to hold good: here it was always assumed that the essence of each mythical figure could be directly learned from its name. The notion that name and essence bear a necessary and internal relation to each other, that the name does not merely denote but actually *is* the essence of its object, that the potency of the real thing is contained in the name—that is one of the fundamental assumptions of the mythmaking consciousness itself. Philosophical and scientific *mythology*, too, seemed to accept this assumption. What in the spirit of myth itself functions as a living and immediate conviction becomes a postulate of reflective procedure for the science of mythology; the doctrine of the intimate relation between names and essences, and of their latent identity, is here set up as a methodological principle.

Among the philosophers it was especially Herbert Spencer who tried to prove the thesis that the mythico-religious veneration of natural phenomena, as, for instance, the sun and the moon, has its ultimate origin in nothing more than a misinterpretation of the *names* which men have applied to these objects. Among the philologists, Max Müller has taken the method of philological analysis not only as a means to reveal the nature of certain mythical beings, especially in the context of Vedic religion, but also as a point of departure for his general theory of the connection between language and myth. For him, myth is neither a transformation of history into fabulous legend nor is it fable accepted as history; and just as certainly it does not spring directly from the contemplation of the great forms and powers of nature. What we call myth is, for him, something conditioned and negotiated by the agency of language; it is, in fact, the product of a basic shortcoming, an inherent weakness of language. All linguistic denotation is essentially ambiguous—and in this ambiguity, this "paronymia" of words lies the source of all myths. The examples by which Max Müller supports this theory are characteristic of his approach. He cites, as one instance, the legend of Deucalion and Pyrrha, who, after Zeus had rescued them from the great flood which destroyed mankind, became the ancestors of a new race by taking up *stones* and casting them over their shoulders, whereupon the stones became men. This origin of human beings from stones is simply absurd and seems to defy all interpretation—but is it not immediately clarified as we recall the fact that in Greek men and stones are denoted by identical or at least similar sounding *names*, that the words λαοί and λᾶας are assonant? Or take the myth of Daphne, who is saved from Apollo's embraces by the fact that her mother, the Earth, transforms her into a laurel tree. Again it is only the history of language that can make this myth "comprehensible," and give it any sort of sense. Who was Daphne? In order to answer this question we must resort to etymology, that is to say, we must investigate the history of the word. "Daphne" can be traced back to the Sanskrit *Ahanâ*, and *Ahanâ* means in Sanskrit the redness of dawn. As soon as we know this, the whole matter becomes clear. The story of Phoebus and Daphne is nothing but a description of what one may observe every day: first, the appearance of the dawnlight in the eastern sky, then the rising of the sun-god who hastens after his bride, then the gradual fading of the red dawn at the touch of the fiery rays, and finally its death or disappearance in the bosom of Mother Earth. So the decisive condition for the development of the myth was not the natural phenomenon itself, but rather the circumstance that the Greek word for the laurel ($\delta\acute{a}\phi\nu\eta$) and the Sanskrit word for the dawn are related; this entails with a sort of logical necessity the identification of the beings they denote. This, therefore, is his conclusion:

"Mythology is inevitable, it is natural, it is an inherent necessity of language, if we recognize in language the outward form and manifestation of thought; it is in fact the dark shadow which language throws upon thought, and which can never disappear till language becomes entirely commensurate with thought, which it never will. Mythology, no doubt, breaks out more fiercely during the early periods of the history of human thought, but it never disappears altogether. Depend upon it, there is mythology now as there was in the time of Homer, only we do not perceive it, because we ourselves live in the very shadow of it, and because we all shrink from the full meridian light of truth. . . . Mythology, in the highest sense, is the power exercised by language on thought in every possible sphere of mental activity."[1]

It might seem an idle pursuit to hark back to such points of view, which have long been abandoned by the etymology and comparative mythological research of to-day, were it not for the fact that this standpoint represents a typical attitude which is ever recurrent in all related fields, in mythology as in linguistic studies, in theory of art as well as in theory of knowledge. For Max Müller the mythical world is essentially a world of illusion—but an illusion that finds its explanation whenever the original, necessary self-deception of the mind, from which the error arises, is discovered. This self-

---

[1] Max Müller, "The Philosophy of Mythology," appended to *Introduction to the Science of Religion* (London, 1873), pp. 353-355.

deception is rooted in language, which is forever making game of the human mind, ever ensnaring it in that iridescent play of meanings that is its own heritage. And this notion that myth does not rest upon a positive power of formulation and creation, but rather upon a mental *defect*—that we find in it a "pathological" influence of speech—this notion has its proponents even in modern ethnological literature.[2]

But when we reduce it to its philosophical lowest terms, this attitude turns out to be simply the logical result of that naïve realism which regards the reality of objects as something directly and unequivocally given, literally something tangible—ἀπρὶξ ταῖν χεροῖν, as Plato says. If reality is conceived in this manner, then of course everything which has not this solid sort of reality dissolves into mere fraud and illusion. This illusion may be ever so finely wrought, and flit about us in the gayest and loveliest colors; the fact remains that this image has no independent content, no intrinsic meaning. It does indeed reflect a reality—but a reality to which it can never measure up, and which it can never adequately portray. From this point of view all artistic creation becomes a mere imitation, which must always fall short of the original. Not only simple imitation of a sensibly presented model, but also what is known as idealization, manner, or style, must finally succumb to this verdict; for measured by the naked "truth" of the object to be depicted, idealization itself is nothing but subjective misconception and falsification. And it seems that all other processes of mental gestation involve the same sort of outrageous distortion, the same departure from objective reality and the immediate data of experience.

[2] E.g., B. Brinton, *Religions of Primitive Peoples* (New York and London, 1907), pp. 115 ff.

For all mental processes fail to grasp reality itself, and in order to represent it, to hold it at all, they are driven to the use of symbols. But all symbolism harbors the curse of mediacy; it is bound to obscure what it seeks to reveal. Thus the sound of speech strives to "express" subjective and objective happening, the "inner" and the "outer" world; but what of this it can retain is not the life and individual fullness of existence, but only a dead abbreviation of it. All that "denotation" to which the spoken word lays claim is really nothing more than mere suggestion; a "suggestion" which, in face of the concrete variegation and totality of actual experience, must always appear a poor and empty shell. That is true of the external as well as the inner world: "When *speaks* the soul, alas, the *soul* no longer speaks!"

From this point it is but a single step to the conclusion which the modern skeptical critics of language have drawn: the complete dissolution of any alleged truth content of language, and the realization that this content is nothing but a sort of phantasmagoria of the spirit. Moreover, from this standpoint, not only myth, art, and language, but even theoretical knowledge itself becomes a phantasmagoria; for even knowledge can never reproduce the true nature of things as they are, but must frame their essence in "concepts." But what are concepts save formulations and creations of thought, which, instead of giving us the true forms of objects, show us rather the forms of thought itself? Consequently all schemata which science evolves in order to classify, organize, and summarize the phenomena of the real world turn out to be nothing but arbitrary schemes— airy fabrics of the mind, which express not the nature of things, but the nature of mind. So knowledge, as well as myth, language, and art, has been reduced to a kind

of fiction—to a fiction that recommends itself by its use-
fulness, but must not be measured by any strict standard
of truth, if it is not to melt away into nothingness.

Against this self-dissolution of the spirit there is only
one remedy: to accept in all seriousness what Kant calls
his "Copernican revolution." Instead of measuring the
content, meaning, and truth of intellectual forms by
something extraneous which is supposed to be reproduced in them, we must find in these forms themselves
the measure and criterion for their truth and intrinsic
meaning. Instead of taking them as mere copies of something else, we must see in each of these spiritual forms
a spontaneous law of generation; an original way and
tendency of expression which is more than a mere record
of something initially given in fixed categories of real
existence. From this point of view, myth, art, language
and science appear as symbols; not in the sense of
mere figures which refer to some given reality by means
of suggestion and allegorical renderings, but in the sense
of forces each of which produces and posits a world of
its own. In these realms the spirit exhibits itself in that
inwardly determined dialectic by virtue of which alone
there is any reality, any organized and definite Being at
all. Thus the special symbolic forms are not imitations,
but *organs* of reality, since it is solely by their agency
that anything real becomes an object for intellectual
apprehension, and as such is made visible to us. The
question as to what reality is apart from these forms, and
what are its independent attributes, becomes irrelevant
here. For the mind, only that can be visible which has
some definite form; but every form of existence has its
source in some peculiar way of seeing, some intellectual
formulation and intuition of meaning. Once language,
myth, art and science are recognized as such ideational

forms, the basic philosophical question is no longer that
of their relation to an absolute reality which forms, so
to speak, their solid and substantial substratum; the central problem now is that of their mutual limitation and
supplementation. Though they all function organically
together in the construction of spiritual reality, yet each
of these organs has its individual assignment.

From this angle, the relation between language and
myth also appears in a new light. It is no longer a matter
of simply deriving one of these phenomena from the
other, of "explaining" it in terms of the other—for
that would be to level them both, to rob them of their
characteristic features. If myth be really, as Max Müller's
theory has it, nothing but the darkening shadow which
language throws upon thought, it is mystifying indeed
that this shadow should appear ever as in an aura of its
own light, should evolve a positive vitality and activity
of its own, which tends to eclipse what we commonly
call the immediate reality of *things*, so that even the
wealth of empirical, sensuous experience pales before it.
As Wilhelm von Humboldt has said in connection with
the language problem: "Man lives with his objects
chiefly—in fact, since his feeling and acting depends on
his perceptions, one may say exclusively—as language
presents them to him. By the same process whereby he
spins language out of his own being, he ensnares himself
in it; and each language draws a magic circle round the
people to which it belongs, a circle from which there is
no escape save by stepping out of it into another."[3]

This holds, perhaps, even more for the basic mythical
conceptions of mankind than for language. Such conceptions are not culled from a ready-made world of

[3] W. von Humboldt, *Einleitung zum Kawi-Werk*, S.W. (Coll. ed.),
VII, 60.

Being, they are not mere products of fantasy which vapor off from fixed, empirical, realistic existence, to float above the actual world like a bright mist; to primitive consciousness they present the *totality* of Being. The mythical form of conception is not something super-added to certain definite *elements* of empirical existence; instead, the primary "experience" itself is steeped in the imagery of myth and saturated with its atmosphere. Man lives with *objects* only in so far as he lives with these *forms*; he reveals reality to himself, and himself to reality, in that he lets himself and the environment enter into this plastic medium, in which the two do not merely make contact, but fuse with each other.

Consequently all those theories which propose to find the roots of myth by exploring the realm of experience, of *objects*, which are supposed to have given rise to it, and from which it then allegedly grew and spread, must always remain one-sided and inadequate. There are, as is well known, a multitude of such explanations—a great variety of doctrines about the ultimate origin and real kernel of mythmaking, hardly less motley than the world of objects itself. Now it is found in certain psychical conditions and experiences, especially the phenomenon of dreaming, now in the contemplation of natural events, and among the latter it is further limited to the observation of natural objects such as the sun, the moon, the stars, or else to that of great occurrences such as storms, lightning and thunder, etc. Thus the attempt is made again and again to make soul mythology or nature mythology, sun or moon or thunder mythology the basis of mythology as such.

But even if one of these attempts should prove successful, this would not solve the real problem which mythology presents to philosophy, but at best would push it back one step. For mythical formulation as such cannot be understood and appreciated simply by determining the *object* on which it is immediately and originally centered. It is, and remains, the same miracle of the spirit and the same mystery, no matter whether it covers this or that realistic matter, whether it deals with the interpretation and articulation of psychical processes or physical things, and in the latter case, just what particular things these may be. Even though it were possible to resolve all mythology to a basic astral mythology—what the mythical consciousness derives from contemplation of the stars, what it sees in them directly, would still be something radically different from the view they present to empirical observation or the way they figure in theoretical speculation and scientific "explanations" of natural phenomena. Descartes said that theoretical science remains the same in its essence no matter what object it deals with—just as the sun's light is the same no matter what wealth and variety of things it may illuminate. The same may be said of any symbolic form, of language, art, or myth, in that each of these is a particular way of seeing, and carries within itself its particular and proper source of light. The function of envisagement, the dawn of a conceptual enlightenment can never be realistically derived from things themselves or understood through the nature of its objective contents. For it is not a question of what we see in a certain perspective, but of the perspective itself. If we conceive the problem in this way, it is certainly clear that a reduction of all myth to one subject matter brings us no nearer to the solution, in fact it removes us further than ever from any hope of a real answer. For now we see in language, art and mythology so many archetypal phenomena of human mentality which can be indicated as such, but

are not capable of any further 'explanation" in terms
of something else. The realists always assume, as their
solid basis for all such explanations, the so-called "given,"
which is thought to have some definite form, some inherent structure of its own. They accept this reality as
an integrated whole of causes and effects, things and attributes, states and processes, of objects at rest and of
motions, and the only question for them is which of
these elements a particular mental product such as myth,
language or art originally embodied. If, for instance, the
phenomenon in question is language, their natural line
of inquiry must be whether names for things preceded
names for conditions or actions, or vice versa—whether,
in other words, nouns or verbs were the first "roots"
of speech. But this problem itself appears spurious as
soon as we realize that the distinctions which here are
taken for granted, the analysis of reality in terms of things
and processes, permanent and transitory aspects, objects
and actions, do not precede language as a substratum of
given fact, but that language itself is what initiates such
articulations, and develops them in its own sphere. Then
it turns out that language could not begin with any
phase of "noun concepts" or "verb concepts," but is the
very agency that produces the distinction between these
forms, that introduces the great spiritual "crisis" in
which the permanent is opposed to the transient, and
Being is made the contrary of Becoming. So the linguistic fundamental concepts must be realized as something prior to these distinctions, forms which lie between the sphere of noun conception and that of verb
conception, between thinghood and eventuality, in a
state of indifference, a peculiar balance of feeling.

A similar ambiguity seems to characterize the earliest

phases to which we can trace back the development of mythical and religious thought. It seems only natural to us that the world should present itself to our inspection and observation as a pattern of definite forms, each with its own perfectly determinate spatial limits that give it its specific individuality. If we see it as a whole, this whole nevertheless consists of clearly distinguishable units, which do not melt into each other, but preserve their identity that sets them definitely apart from the identity of all the others. But for the mythmaking consciousness these separate elements are not thus separately given, but have to be originally and gradually derived from the whole; the process of culling and sorting out individual forms has yet to be gone through. For this reason the mythic state of mind has been called the "complex" state, to distinguish it from our abstract analytic attitude. Preuss, who coined this expression, points out, for instance, that in the mythology of the Cora Indians, which he has studied exhaustively, the conception of the nocturnal heaven and the diurnal heaven must have preceded that of the sun, the moon, and the separate constellations. The first mythical impulse, he claims, was not toward making a sun-god or a lunar deity, but a community of stars. "The sun-god does indeed hold first rank in the hierarchy of the gods, but . . . the various astral deities can stand proxy for him. They precede him in time, he is created by them, by somebody's jumping into a fire or being thrown into it; his power is influenced by theirs, and he is artificially kept alive by feeding on the hearts of sacrificed victims, i.e., the stars. The starry night sky is the necessary condition for the existence of the sun; that is the central idea in the whole religious ideation of the Coras and of the

ancient Mexicans, and must be regarded as a principal
factor in the further development of their religion."[4]

The same function here attributed to the nocturnal
heavens seems to be imputed by the Indo-Germanic
races to the daylit sky. Their religions show many traces
of the fact that the worship of light as an undifferentiated, total experience preceded that of the individual
heavenly bodies, which figure only as its media, its particular manifestations. In the Avesta, for instance, Mithra
is not a sun-god, as he is for later ages; he is the spirit
of heavenly light. He appears on the mountaintops
before the sun rises, to mount his chariot which, drawn
by four white horses, runs the course of heaven during
the day; when night comes, he the unsleeping still lights
the face of earth with a vague glimmering light. We are
explicitly told that he is neither the sun, nor the moon,
nor any or all of the stars, but through them, his thousand ears and ten thousand eyes, he perceives everything and keeps watch over the world.[5]

Here we see in a concrete instance how mythic conception originally grasps only the great, fundamental,
qualitative contrast of light and darkness, and how it
treats them as one essence, one complex whole, out of
which definite characters only gradually emerge. Like
the spirit of language, the mythmaking genius "has"
separate and individualized forms only in so far as it
"posits" them, as it carves them out of the undifferentiated whole of its pristine vision.

This insight into the determining and discriminating
function, which myth as well as language performs in

[4] Preuss, *Die Nayarit-Expedition I: Die Religion der Cora Indianer*,
Leipzig, 1912. Cf. further, Preuss, *Die geistige Kultur der Naturvölker*,
pp. 9 ff.
[5] Yasht X, 145; Yasna I, ii (35); cf. Cumont, *Textes et monuments
figurés relatifs aux mystères de Mithra* (Brussels, 1899), I, p. 225.

the mental construction of our world of "things", seems to be all that a "philosophy of symbolic forms" can teach us. Philosophy as such can go no further; it cannot presume to present to us, *in concreto*, the great process of emergence, and to distinguish its phases for us. But if pure philosophy is necessarily restricted to a general, theoretical picture of such an evolution, it may be that philology and comparative mythology can fill in the outline and draw with firm, clear strokes what philosophical speculation could only suggestively sketch. An initial and portentous step in this direction has been taken by Usener in his work on divine names. "An Essay toward a Science of Religious Conception," is the subtitle he has given to his book, which brings it definitely into the realm of philosophical problems and systematic treatment. To trace the history of the divinities, their successive appearance and development among the several tribes of man, he tells us, is not an attainable goal; only a history of mythic ideas can be reconstructed. Such ideas, no matter how manifold, how varied, how heterogeneous they may appear at first sight, have their own inner lawfulness; they do not arise from a boundless caprice of the imagination, but move in definite avenues of feeling and creative thought. This intrinsic law is what mythology seeks to establish. Mythology is the science (λόγος) of myth, or the science of the forms of religious conception.[6]

His findings in this field may certainly give pause to philosophers, who tend to regard the human mind as endowed *ab initio* with logical categories. "There have been long periods in mental evolution," he observes, "when the human mind was slowly laboring toward thought and conception and was following quite differ-

---

[6] Usener, *Götternamen. Versuch einer Lehre von der religiösen Begriffsbildung* (Bonn, 1896), p. 330; cf. esp. pp. v ff.

ent laws of ideation and speech. Our epistemology will
not have any real foundation until philology and mythology have revealed the processes of involuntary and unconscious conception. The chasm between specific perception and general concepts is far greater than our
academic notions, and a language which does our thinking for us, lead us to suppose. It is so great that I cannot
imagine how it could have been bridged, had not language itself, without man's conscious awareness, prepared and induced the process. It is language that causes
the multitude of casual, individual expressions to yield
up one which extends its denotation over more and more
special cases, until it comes to denote them all, and assumes the power of expressing a class concept" (p. 321).

Here, then, it is the philologist, the student of language and religion, who confronts philosophy with a new
question, which emerges from his own investigations.
And Usener has not merely indicated a new approach;
he has resolutely followed it up, employing to this end
all the clues which the history of language, the precise
analysis of words, and especially that of divine names
provided. The question naturally arises whether philosophy, not commanding any such materials, can handle
this problem which the humanistic sciences have presented to it, and what intellectual resources it can tap
to meet such a challenge. Is there any other line than
the actual *history* of language and of religion that could
lead us closer to the origin of primary linguistic and
religious concepts? Or is it, at this point, one and the
same thing to know the genesis of such ideas and to
know their ultimate meanings and functions? This is
the issue I propose to decide in the following pages. I
shall take up Usener's problem in exactly the form in
which he has cast it; but I shall attempt to tackle it on

other grounds than linguistic and philological considerations. Usener himself has indicated the propriety, in fact the necessity of such an approach, in that he formulated the main issue as not merely a matter of linguistic and intellectual history, but also of logic and epistemology. This presupposes that the latter disciplines, too, can handle the problem of semantic and mythic conception from their own standpoint, and treat it by their own methodological principles and procedures. Through this expansion, this apparent overstepping of the usual boundaries of logical inquiry, the science of logic really comes into its own, and the realm of pure theoretical reason becomes actually defined and distinguished from other spheres of intellectual being and development.

⋖§ 2 §⋗

The Evolution of Religious Ideas

BEFORE we move, however, to the attack on this general objective, we must grasp the separate facts which Usener's studies in the history of language and religion have brought to light, in order to have a concrete basis for our theoretical interpretations and constructions. In the evolution of those theological concepts which he has traced by means of divine nomenclatures he distinguishes three principal phases. The oldest of these is marked by the production of "momentary deities." These beings do not personify any force of nature, nor do they represent some special aspect of human life; no recurrent trait or value is retained in them and transformed into a

mythico-religious image; it is something purely instan-
taneous, a fleeting, emerging and vanishing mental content, whose objectification and outward discharge
produces the image of the "momentary deity." Every impression that man receives, every wish that stirs in him,
every hope that lures him, every danger that threatens
him can affect him thus religiously. Just let spontaneous
feeling invest the object before him, or his own personal
condition, or some display of power that surprises him,
with an air of holiness, and the momentary god has been
experienced and created. In stark uniqueness and single-
ness it confronts us; not as a part of some force which
may manifest itself here, there and everywhere, in various places and times, and for different persons, but as
something that exists only here and now, in one indivis-
ible moment of experience, and for only one subject
whom it overwhelms and holds in thrall.

Usener has shown through examples of Greek literature how real this primitive religious feeling was even
in the Greeks of the classic period, and how it activated
them again and again. "By reason of this vivacity and
responsiveness of their religious sentiment, any idea or
object which commands, for the moment, their undivided interest, may be exalted to divine status: Reason and Understanding, Wealth, Chance, Climax, Wine,
Feasting, or the body of the Beloved. . . . Whatever
comes to us suddenly like a sending from heaven, whatever rejoices or grieves or oppresses us, seems to the
religious consciousness like a divine being. As far back
as we can trace the Greeks, they subsume such experiences under the generic term of δαίμων" (pp. 290f).

On a somewhat higher plane than these momentary
daemons, which come and go, appearing and dissolving
like the subjective emotions from which they arise, we

find a new series of divinities, originating not from spontaneous feelings, but from the ordered and continual activities of mankind. As intellectual and cultural development progresses, our relation toward the outer world changes proportionately from a passive to an active attitude. Man ceases to be a mere shuttlecock at the mercy of outward impressions and influences; he exercises his own will to direct the course of events according to his needs and wishes. This course now has its own measure and periodicity: at definite intervals, in uniform cycles from day to day and month to month, human activities repeat themselves and are linked with invariant, permanent effects. But again the human ego can realize its present activity, as formerly its passivity, only by projecting it into the outer world, and giving it some concrete form. So every department of human activity gives rise to a particular deity that represents it. These deities, too, which Usener calls "special gods" (Sondergötter), have as yet no general function and significance; they do not permeate existence in its whole depth and scope, but are limited to a mere section of it, a narrowly circumscribed department. But within their respective spheres they have attained to permanence and definite character, and therewith to a certain generality. The patron god of harrowing, for instance, the god Occator, rules not only this year's harrowing, or the cultivation of a particular field, but is the god of harrowing in general, who is annually invoked by the whole community as its helper and protector upon the recurrence of this agricultural practice. So he represents a special and perhaps a humble rustic activity, but he represents it in its generality (p. 280).

Usener demonstrates, through the so-called "functional gods" of the Romans, how widely and variously this type of special deity is developed in Roman religion. Every practical performance has its patron: the first breaking of fallow soil, the second plowing, the acts of sowing, of weeding, the cutting of the grain and likewise the harvesting; and none of these undertakings can be successful unless its appropriate god has been invoked in prescribed fashion and by his correct name. Usener has uncovered the same structure of the popular pantheon according to separate activities in Lithuanian tradition. From this as well as from similar findings in the history of Greek religion he draws the conclusion that the natures and names of such deities turn up at a certain stage of religious development among all peoples. They represent a necessary phase which religious consciousness must traverse in order to reach its final and supreme achievement, the conception of personal gods. The process, however, whereby it attains this goal can be revealed, according to Usener, only by philological research; for "the necessary condition for the genesis of personal gods is a linguistic-historical process" (p. 316). Whenever a special god is first conceived, it is invested with a special name, which is derived from the particular activity that has given rise to the deity. As long as this name is understood, and taken in its original sense, the limits of its meaning are the limits of the god's powers; through his name the god is permanently held to that narrow field for which he was originally created. Quite otherwise, however, if through an accident of phonetic changes or the obsolescence of its verbal root the name loses its meaning and its connection with the living language. Then the name no longer suggests to those who use it the idea of a *single* activity, to which the subject that bears it must be exclusively bound. The word has become a proper name—and this connotes, just like the given name of a man, the conception of a *personality*. Thus a new Being has been produced, which continues to develop by a law of its own. The concept of the special god, which expressed a certain activity rather than a certain nature, now achieves its embodiment and appears, so to speak, in the flesh. This god is now capable of acting and suffering like a human creature; he engages in all sorts of actions, and instead of being wholly consummated in one function he is related to it as an independent subject. The many divine names which originally denoted a corresponding number of sharply distinguished special gods now fuse in one personality, which has thus emerged; they become the several appellations of this Being, expressing various aspects of his nature, power and range (pp. 301f., 325, 330).

What intrigues us about these results of Usener's, which we have tried to recapitulate in brief, is not primarily his material conclusion but the method by which he has arrived at it. That method is summed up in his preface with these words: "Only through devoted preoccupation with the spiritual traces of vanished times, that is to say, through philological research, can we train ourselves to feel with the past; then gradually sympathetic strains may be set in motion within us so that we find in our own consciousness the threads that link ancient and modern times. A greater wealth of observation and comparison allows us to go further and proceed from the particular case to a law. It would be a sad pass for human knowledge if detailed research *ipso facto* fettered the mind and prevented it from seeking a synoptic vision. The deeper you delve, the more you may expect to be rewarded by general insight."

Usener draws most of his material evidence from the history of Greek and Roman religion; yet he makes it

perfectly clear that these demonstrations are merely
representative instances of a pattern that is generally
valid. Indeed, he specifically admits and stresses the fact
that he gained his understanding of many important,
basic traits in Graeco-Roman religion only through his
extensive studies of Lithuanian paganism. And even in
entirely unrelated fields, in American and African systems of belief, there are often astonishing parallels which
serve to support and illuminate his fundamental theses
in religious history and philosophy. In the detailed and
careful account of the Evé tribe which Spieth has published there is a description of Evé gods that is nothing
short of a paragon of what Usener has introduced under
the name of "momentary deities."

"After the inhabitants of the town of Dzake in Peki
had settled that place, a certain farmer at work in his
fields went to look for water. In a trough-shaped hollow
he drove his machete into the damp soil. Suddenly a
gory looking stream welled up before him, of which he
drank, and which he found refreshing. He told his family
about it and persuaded them to come with him and worship that red fluid. After a while the water cleared, and
all the family drank of it. From this time on, this water
was a trō to its discoverer and to his kin. . . .

"It is said that upon the arrival of the first settlers of
Anvlo a man happened to be standing before a great,
thick breadfruit tree. At the sight of the tree, he felt
panicky. He went to the priest to ask for an explanation
of this event. The answer he received was that the tree
was a trō which wanted to live with him and be wor-
shipped by him. So his fright was the sign whereby the
man knew that a trō had revealed itself to him. . . . If
anyone takes refuge in an anthill from his human or
animal persecutors, he will say afterwards: 'The anthill

saved my life.' It is the same when a man finds safety in a brook from some raging wounded animal, or a family or entire clan takes shelter from the enemy in some mountain fastness. In every case the rescue is ascribed to some indwelling power of the object or place where, or by means of which, it occurred."[7]

The value of such observations for the general history of religions lies in the fact that here a dynamic concept of deity has taken the place of the static ones with which both are wont to operate; that the god or daemon is not merely described according to his nature and significance, but that the law of his origin is taken into consideration. An attempt is made to spy out his genesis from the mythico-religious consciousness, in fact to note the very hour of his birth. If empirical science, in the realms of etymology, religion and ethnology, finds itself faced with problems of this sort, surely no one can deny philosophy the right to essay them, and bring its own principles and interests to bear on their solution.

◆§ 3 §◆

Language and Conception

TO know and understand the peculiar nature of mythico-religious conception not only through its results, but through the very principle of its formation, and to see,

---

[7] Spieth, *Die Religion der Eweer in Süd-Togo* (Leipzig, 1911), pp. 7f; cf. esp. Spieth's work on the Evé tribes (Berlin, 1906), pp. 462, 480, 490.—The examples here given are especially suited for refutation of Wundt's objection that Usener's "momentary gods" are "not really empirical data but rather logical postulates" (*Volkspsychologie*, IV, 561).

furthermore, how the growth of linguistic concepts is related to that of religious ideas and in what essential traits they coincide—this requires us, indeed, to reach far back into the past. We must not hesitate to take a roundabout way through general logic and epistemology, for it is only upon this basis that we may hope to determine precisely the *function* of this sort of ideation and to distinguish it clearly from the conceptual forms which serve theoretical thinking. According to the traditional teachings of logic, the mind forms concepts by taking a certain number of objects which have common properties, i.e., coincide in certain respects, together in thought and abstracting from their differences, so that only the similarities are retained and reflected upon, and in this way a general idea of such-and-such a class of objects is formed in consciousness. Thus the concept (*notio, conceptus*) is that idea which represents the totality of *essential* properties, i.e., the *essence* of the objects in question. In this apparently simple and obvious explanation, everything depends on what one means by a "property," and how such properties are supposed to be originally determined. The formulation of a general concept presupposes *definite* properties; only if there are fixed characteristics by virtue of which things may be recognized as similar or dissimilar, coinciding or not coinciding, is it possible to collect objects which resemble each other into a class. But—we cannot help asking at this point—how can such differentiae exist prior to language? Do we not, rather, *realize* them only by means of language, through the very act of naming them? And if the latter be the case, then by what rules and what criteria is this act carried out? What is it that leads or constrains language to collect just *these* ideas into a single whole and denote them by a word? What causes it to select, from the ever-flowing, ever-uniform stream of impressions which strike our senses or arise from the autonomous processes of the mind, certain pre-eminent forms, to dwell on them and endow them with a particular "significance"? As soon as we cast the problem in this mold, traditional logic offers no support to the student and philosopher of language; for its explanation of the origin of generic concepts presupposes the very thing we are seeking to understand and derive—the formulation of linguistic notions.[8] The problem becomes even more difficult, as well as more urgent, if one considers that the form of that ideational synthesis which leads to the primary verbal concepts and denotations is not simply and unequivocally determined by the object itself, but allows scope for the free operation of language and for its specific mental stamp. Of course, even this freedom must have its rules, and this original, creative power has a law of its own. Can this law be set forth, and can it be brought into relation with the principles that govern other spheres of spiritual expression, especially the rules of mythical, religious, and purely theoretical, i.e., scientific, conception?

Beginning with the last of these branches, we can show that all the intellectual labor whereby the mind forms general concepts out of specific impressions is directed toward breaking the isolation of the datum, wresting it from the "here and now" of its actual occurrence, relating it to other things and gathering it and them into some inclusive order, into the unity of a "system." The logical form of conception, from the standpoint of theoretical knowledge, is nothing but a preparation for the logical form of judgment; all judg-

[8] For more detailed discussion of this point see my *Philosophie der symbolischen Formen*, I, 244ff.

ment, however, aims at overcoming the illusion of singularity which adheres to every particular content of consciousness. The apparently singular fact becomes known, understood and conceptually grasped only in so far as it is "subsumed" under a general idea, recognized as a "case" of a law or as a member of a manifold or a series. In this sense every genuine judgment is synthetic; for what it intends and strives for is just this synthesis of parts into a whole, this weaving of particulars into a system. This synthesis cannot be achieved immediately and at a single stroke; it has to be worked out step by step, by a progressive activity of relating separate notions or sense impressions with each other, and then gathering up the resultant wholes into greater complexes, until finally the union of all these separate complexes yields the coherent picture of the totality of things. The will to this totality is the vivifying principle of our theoretical and empirical conception. This principle, therefore, is necessarily "discursive"; that is to say, it starts with a particular case, but instead of dwelling upon it, and resting content in sheer contemplation of the particular, it lets the mind merely start from this instance to run the whole gamut of Being in the special directions determined by the empirical concept. By this process of running through a realm of experience, i.e., of discursive thinking, the particular receives its fixed intellectual "meaning" and definite character. It has different appearances according to the ever-broadening contexts in which it is taken; the place it holds in the totality of Being, or rather the place which the progressive march of thought assigns to it, determines its content and its theoretical significance.

How this ideal of knowledge controls the rise of science, especially the construction of mathematical physics, requires no further elucidation. All the concepts of physics have no other aim than to transform the "rhapsody of perceptions," by which the world of sense is actually presented to us, into a system, a coherent epitome of laws. Each individual datum becomes a phenomenon and object of "nature" only as it meets this requirement—for "nature" in the theoretical sense, according to the Kantian definition, is nothing but the existence of things as determined by general laws.

A distinction has often been drawn between the "individualizing" mode of historical thought and the "generalizing" mode of science. While in the latter any concrete case is merely regarded as an instance of a general law, and while the "here" and "now" has no significance save in so far as it reveals a universal rule, it is said that history deliberately seeks out this here and now, in order to grasp it ever more precisely in just this character. But even in historical thinking the particular fact is significant only by virtue of the relationships into which it enters. Although it cannot be regarded as an instance of a general law, yet in order to be historically conceived, to appear *sub specie* the mode of history, it must take its place as a *member* of a course of events or belong to some teleological nexus. Its determination in time is the exact opposite of its temporal separateness; for historically it has meaning only if and as it refers back to a past and forward to a future. Thus all genuine historical reflection, instead of losing itself in contemplation of the merely singular and nonrecurrent, must strive, like the morphological thought of Goethe, to find those "pregnant" moments in the course of events where, as in focal points, whole series of occurrences are epitomized. In such points, phases of reality that are temporally widely separated become connected and linked for historical conception and understanding. As certain high moments are culled from the uniform stream of time, and are related to each other, and concatenated in series, the origin and end of all happenings, their whence and whither, is gradually illumined. So historical conception, too, is characterized by the fact that through it a thousand connections are forged by one stroke; and it is not so much the contemplation of particulars as an awareness of such relationships that constitutes the peculiar historicity, or what we call the historical significance of facts.

But let us not dwell longer on such general observations, because our concern is not primarily with the structure of scientific concepts; we are considering this structure only in order to clarify another, namely, the form and character of the primordial linguistic concepts. While this remains to be done, the purely logical theory of conception cannot be completely developed. For all the concepts of theoretical knowledge constitute merely an upper stratum of logic which is founded upon a lower stratum, that of the logic of language. Before the intellectual work of conceiving and understanding of phenomena can set in, the work of *naming* must have preceded it, and have reached a certain point of elaboration. For it is this process which transforms the world of sense impression, which animals also possess, into a mental world, a world of ideas and meanings. All theoretical cognition takes its departure from a world already preformed by language; the scientist, the historian, even the philosopher, lives with his objects only as language presents them to him. This immediate dependence is harder to realize than anything that the mind creates mediately, by conscious thought processes. It is easy to see that logical theory, which traces concepts back to

an act of generalizing "abstraction," is of little use here;
for this "abstraction" consists of selecting from the
wealth of *given* properties certain ones which are common to several sensory or intuitive experiences; but our
problem is not the choice of properties already given,
but the *positing* of the properties themselves. It is to
comprehend and illuminate the nature and direction of
noticing, which must precede mentally the function of
"denoting." Even those thinkers who have concerned
themselves most actively with the problem of the
"origin of language" have thought it necessary to stop
at this point, and have simply assumed a "faculty" of
the soul for the process of "noticing."

"When man attained that condition of reflection
which is peculiar to him," says Herder in his essay on
the origins of language, "and when this reflection first
achieved free play, he invented speech." Suppose a certain animal, say a lamb, to pass before the eyes of a
human being: what image, what view of it will present
itself to him? Not the same that would arise for wolves
or lions; they would smell and taste it mentally, be over-
come by sensuality, and instinct would throw them upon
it. Nor would man's image be like that of another animal
to whom the lamb was of no direct interest; for such an
animal would let it glide vaguely past, because its own
instinct was turned in another direction. "But with man,
not so! As soon as he is in a position to become ac-
quainted with the lamb, there is no instinct to interfere
with him; there is no sensuality to draw him into too
close contact with it, or to repel him from it; it stands
before him just as it meets his senses. White, gentle,
woolly—his mind in its conscious exercise seeks a characteristic for it—the lamb bleats! He has found the differentia. His inner sense is activated. This bleating,

which has made the liveliest impression on his mind, that freed itself from all other properties of sight and touch, stood forth, and entered most deeply into his experience—'Ah! You are the bleating one!'—remains with him; he feels that he has recognized it *humanly*, has interpreted it, in that he knows it by a property. . . . By a property, then? And is that anything but by an inward *denoting word?* The sound of bleating, thus apprehended by a human being as the character of the sheep, became, through the medium of reflection, the *name* of the sheep, even though his tongue had never attempted to utter it."[9]

In these statements of Herder's one can still hear quite clearly the echoes of those theories which he was combating—the traces of the language theories of the Enlightenment, which derived language from conscious reflection and considered it as something "invented." Man looks for a differentia because he needs it; because his reason, his specific faculty of "reflection" demands it. This demand itself remains something underived—a "basic power of the soul." Thus the explanation has really progressed in a circle: for the end and goal of language formation, the act of denotation by specific properties, must be regarded as also the principle of its beginning.

Humboldt's notion of the "inward form of language" seems to lead in another direction. For he no longer considers the "whence" of linguistic concepts, but is concerned purely with their "what"; not their origin, but the demonstration of their character constitutes his problem. The form of observation, which underlies all speech and language development, always expresses a peculiar spiritual character, a special way of conceiving

[9] "Ueber den Ursprung der Sprache," *Werke* (ed. Supham), V, 35f.

and apprehending. The difference between the several
languages, therefore, is not a matter of different sounds
and marks, but of different world conceptions. If the
moon is denoted in Greek as the Measuring One ($\mu\acute{\eta}\nu$),
in Latin as the Shining One (luna), or if even in one
and the same language, as in Sanskrit, the elephant is
called now the Twice Drinker, now the Two-Tusked
One, now the Handed One—that goes to show that
language never denotes simply objects, things as such,
but always conceptions arising from the autonomous
activity of the mind. The nature of concepts, therefore,
depends on the way this active viewing is directed.

But even this notion of the inward form of language
really has to presuppose that which it professes to prove
and reveal. For, on the one hand, speech is here the
vehicle of any world perspective, the medium through
which thought must pass before it can find itself and
assume a definite theoretical form; but, on the other
hand, just this sort of form, this definite perspective has
to be presupposed, in order to explain the particular
character of any given language, its special way of seeing
and denoting. So the question of the origin of language
tends always to become—even for the thinkers who have
taken it most profoundly and struggled hardest with
it—a veritable monkey puzzle. All the energy devoted
to it seems only to lead us about in a circle and finally
leave us at the point from which we started.

And yet the very nature of such fundamental problems entails that the mind, though it despairs of ever
finally solving them, can never quite let them alone.
And we receive something like a new hope of a solution
if, instead of comparing the primary linguistic forms
with the forms of logical conception, we try to compare
them with those of mythical ideation. What holds these

two kinds of conception, the linguistic and the mythical, together in one category, and opposes both of them to the form of logical thought, is the fact that they both seem to reveal the same sort of intellectual apprehension, which runs counter to that of our theoretical thought processes. The aim of theoretical thinking, as we have seen, is primarily to deliver the contents of sensory or intuitive experience from the isolation in which they originally occur. It causes these contents to transcend their narrow limits, combines them with others, compares them, and concatenates them in a definite order, in an all-inclusive context. It proceeds "discursively," in that it treats the immediate content only as a point of departure, from which it can run the whole gamut of impressions in various directions, until these impressions are fitted together into one unified conception, one closed system. In this system there are no more isolated points; all its members are reciprocally related, refer to one another, illumine and explain each other. Thus every separate event is ensnared, as it were, by invisible threads of thought, that bind it to the whole. The theoretical significance which it receives lies in the fact that it is stamped with the character of this totality.

Mythical thinking, when viewed in its most elementary forms, bears no such stamp; in fact, the character of intellectual unity is directly hostile to its spirit. For in this mode, thought does not dispose freely over the data of intuition, in order to relate and compare them to each other, but is captivated and enthralled by the intuition which suddenly confronts it. It comes to rest in the immediate experience; the sensible present is so great that everything else dwindles before it. For a person whose apprehension is under the spell of this mythico-religious attitude, it is as though the whole world were simply annihilated; the immediate content, whatever it be, that commands his religious interest so completely fills his consciousness that nothing else can exist beside and apart from it. The ego is spending all its energy on this single object, lives in it, loses itself in it. Instead of a widening of intuitive experience, we find here its extreme limitation; instead of expansion that would lead through greater and greater spheres of being, we have here an impulse toward concentration; instead of extensive distribution, intensive compression. This focusing of all forces on a single point is the prerequisite for all mythical thinking and mythical formulation. When, on the one hand, the entire self is given up to a single impression, is "possessed" by it and, on the other hand, there is the utmost tension between the subject and its object, the outer world; when external reality is not merely viewed and contemplated, but overcomes a man in sheer immediacy, with emotions of fear or hope, terror or wish fulfillment: then the spark jumps somehow across, the tension finds release, as the subjective excitement becomes objectified, and confronts the mind as a god or a daemon.

Here we have the mythico-religious protophenomenon which Usener has sought to fix with the term "momentary god." "In absolute immediacy," he says, "the individual phenomenon is deified, without the intervention of even the most rudimentary class concept; that one thing which you see before you, that and nothing else is the god" (p. 280). To this day, the life of primitive races shows us certain features in which this process is almost tangibly clear. We may recall the examples of it which Spieth adduces: wafer found by a thirsty person, a termite mound that hides and saves someone, any new object that inspires a man with sudden terror—all these are transformed directly into gods. Spieth summarizes his observations with the words: "To the mind of the Evé, the moment in which an object or any striking attributes of it enter into any noticeable relation, pleasant or unpleasant, with the life and spirit of man, that moment a Trō is born in his consciousness." It is as though the isolated occurrence of an impression, its separation from the totality of ordinary, commonplace experience produced not only a tremendous intensification, but also the highest degree of *condensation*, and as though by virtue of this condensation the objective form of the god were created so that it veritably burst forth from the experience.

Now it is here, in this intuitive creative form of myth, and not in the formation of our discursive theoretical concepts, that we must look for the key which may unlock for us the secrets of the original conceptions of language. The formulation of language, too, should not be traced back to any sort of reflective contemplation, to the calm and clearheaded comparison of given sense impressions and the abstraction of definite attributes; but here again we must abandon this static point of view for the comprehension of the dynamic process which produces the verbal sound out of its own inner drive. To be sure, this retrospect in itself is not enough; for through it we are merely brought to the further, more difficult question, how it is possible for anything permanent to result from such a dynamism, and why the vague billowing and surging of sensory impressions and feelings should give rise to an objective, verbal "structure." The modern science of language, in its efforts to elucidate the "origin" of language, has indeed gone back frequently to Hamann's dictum, that poetry is "the mother-tongue of humanity"; its scholars have emphasized the fact that speech is rooted not in the prosaic, but in the poetic aspect of life, so that its ultimate basis must be sought not in preoccupation with the objective view of things and their classification according to certain attributes, but in the primitive power of subjective feeling.[10] But although this doctrine may seem, at first sight, to evade the vicious circle into which the theory of logical expression is ever lapsing, in the end it also cannot bridge the gulf between the purely denotative and the expressive function of speech. In this theory, too, there always remains a sort of hiatus between the lyrical aspect of verbal expression and its logical character; what remains obscure is exactly that *emancipation* whereby a sound is transformed from an emotional utterance into a denotative one.

Here we may be guided once more by consideration of how the "momentary gods" were generated. If such a god is, in his origin, the creation of a moment, if he owes his existence to some entirely concrete and individual, never-recurring situation, he yet achieves a certain substantiality which lifts him far above this accidental condition of his origin. Once he has been divorced from the immediate exigency, the fear or hope of the moment, he becomes an independent being, which henceforth lives on by a law of its own, and has gained form and continuity. He appears to men not as a creature of the hour, but as an objective and superior power, which they adore and which their cult endows with more and more definite form. The image of the momentary god, instead of merely preserving the memory of what he originally meant and was—a deliverance from fear,

[10] See Otto Jespersen, *Progress in Language* (London, 1894), esp. pp. 332 ff.

the fulfillment of a wish and a hope—persists and remains long after that memory has faded and finally
disappeared altogether.

The same function which the image of the god performs, the same tendency to permanent existence, may
be ascribed to the uttered sounds of language. The
word, like a god or a daemon, confronts man not as a
creation of his own, but as something existent and significant in its own right, as an objective reality. As soon
as the spark has jumped across, as soon as the tension
and emotion of the moment has found its discharge in
the word or the mythical image, a sort of turning point
has occurred in human mentality: the inner excitement
which was a mere subjective state has vanished, and has
been resolved into the objective form of myth or of
speech. And now an ever-progressive objectification can
begin. In the same measure in which the autonomous
activity of man extends over a widening sphere, and becomes adjusted and organized within that sphere, his
mythical and verbal *world* undergoes a progressive organization and ever more definite articulation. The
"momentary gods" are succeeded by gods of activity, as
Usener has shown us through the examples of the Roman
"functional gods" and the corresponding Lithuanian
deities. Wissowa summarizes the basic character of
Roman religion with the words: "All their deities are
entirely practically conceived, so to speak—conceived as
being effective in those things with which the Roman
dealt in his ordinary life: the local environment in which
he moved, the various occupations in which he engaged,
the occasions that determine and shape the life of the
individual as well as the community—all these things
are in the keeping of clearly conceived gods with definitely recognized powers. For the Roman, even Jupiter

and Tellus were gods of the Roman community, gods of the hearth and the heath, of wood and wold, seedtime and harvest, of growth and flower and fruit."[11] Here one can trace directly how humanity really attains its insight into objective reality only through the medium of its own activity and the progressive differentiation of that activity; before man thinks in terms of logical concepts, he holds his experiences by means of clear, separate, mythical images. And here, too, the development of language appears to be the counterpart of the development which mythical intuition and thought undergo; for one cannot grasp the true nature and function of linguistic concepts if one regards them as copies, as representations of a definite world of facts, whose components are given to the human mind *ab initio* in stark and separate outlines. Again, the limits of things must first be posited, the outlines drawn, by the agency of language; and this is accomplished as man's activity becomes internally organized, and his conception of Being acquires a correspondingly clear and definite pattern.

We have already demonstrated that the primary function of linguistic concepts does not consist in the comparison of experiences and the selection of certain common attributes, but in the concentration of such experiences, so to speak, in distilling them down to one point. But the manner of this concentration always depends upon the direction of the subject's interest, and is determined not so much by the content of the experience as by the teleological perspective from which it is viewed. Whatever appears important for our wishing and willing, our hope and anxiety, for acting and doing: that and only that receives the stamp of verbal "meaning." Dis-

[11] G. Wissowa, *Religion und Kultus der Römer* (Munich, 1912), Vol. 2, pp. 24f.

tinctions in meaning are the prerequisite for that solidi-
fication of impressions which, as we said above, is a
necessary condition for their denotation by words. For
only what is related somehow to the focus point of willing
and doing, only what proves to be essential to the whole
scheme of life and activity, is selected from the uniform
flux of sense impressions, and is "noticed" in the midst
of them—that is to say, receives a special linguistic accent, a name. The beginnings of this process of "noticing" must undoubtedly be attributed even to animal
mentality; for in their world of experience, too, those
elements upon which their impulses and instincts center
are singled out by their conscious apprehension. Only
something that arouses a single impulse, such as the
nutritional or the sexual impulse, or anything that relates to it, "is there" for an animal as an objective content of its feeling and apperception. But such a presence
always fills just the actual moment in which the impulse
is evoked, is directly stimulated. As soon as the excitation abates, and the desire is fulfilled, the world of Being,
the order of perceptions collapses again. When a new
stimulus reaches the animal's consciousness, this world
may be resurrected; but it is always held in the narrow
confines of actual drives and excitations. Its successive
beginnings always fill just the present moment, without
ranging themselves in any progression; the past is but
dimly retained, the future does not become an image, a
prospect. Only symbolic expression can yield the possibility of prospect and retrospect, because it is only by
symbols that distinctions are not merely *made*, but *fixed*
in consciousness. What the mind has once created, what
has been culled from the total sphere of consciousness,
does not fade away again when the spoken word has set
its seal upon it and given it definite form.

Here, too, the recognition of function precedes that of Being. The aspects of Being are distinguished and co-ordinated according to a measure supplied by action— hence they are guided, not by any "objective" similarity among things, but by their appearance through the medium of practice, which relates them within a purposive nexus. This teleological character of verbal concepts may be readily supported and clarified by means of examples from the history of language.[12] A great many of the phenomena which philologists commonly treat under the general heading of "changes of meaning" can really be understood in principle only from this angle. If altered conditions of life, the changes that attend the advance of culture, have brought men into a new practical relation with their environment, the concepts inherent in language do not retain their original "sense." They begin to shift, to move about, in the same measure as the bounds of human activity tend to vary and efface each other. Wherever, for any reason, the distinction between two activities loses its importance and meaning, there is wont to be a corresponding shift of verbal meanings, namely, of the words which marked that distinction. A very characteristic instance of this sort of thing may be found in an article which Meinhof has published under the title, "On the Influence of Occupation on the Language of the Bantu Tribes in Africa." According to Meinhof, "The Herero have a word, *rima*, to denote sowing, which is phonetically identical with *lima*, the word for hoeing, cultivating, in other Bantu languages. The reason for this peculiar change of meaning is that the Herero neither sow nor cultivate the ground. They are cowherds, and their whole vocabulary

---

[12] In regard to the "teleological" structure of language, cf. the more detailed study in my *Philosophie d. symbolischen Formen*, I, 254ff.

smells of cows. Sowing and cultivating they deem unworthy occupations for a man; so they do not find it worth while to draw nice distinctions among such inferior tasks."[13]

Primitive languages especially furnish many further examples in support of the principle that the order of nomenclature does not rest on the external similarities among things or events, but that different items bear the same name, and are subsumed under the same concept, whenever their *functional* significance is the same, i.e., whenever they hold the same place or at least analogous places in the order of human activities and purposes. Certain Indian tribes, for instance, are said to use the same word for "dancing" and for "working"[14]—obviously because the distinction between these two activities is not immediately apparent to them, since in their scheme of things dance and agriculture serve essentially the same purpose of providing the means of livelihood. The growth and prosperity of their crops seems to them to depend as much or more on the correct performance of their dances, their magical and religious ceremonies, than on prompt and proper attention to the soil.[15] Such a fusion of activities gives rise to the identification of their respective names, the "concepts" of language. When the natives along the Swan River in Africa were first introduced to the sacrament of Communion, they called it a dance;[16] which goes further to show how a unity may

[13] "Ueber die Einwirkung der Beschäftigung auf die Sprache bei den Bantustämmen Afrikas," *Globus*, Vol. 75 (1899), p. 361.

[14] "Die Tarahumara tanzen überhaupt nur zu Zauberzwecken bzw. als 'Gebet.' Tanzen ist ihnen daher . . . gleich arbeiten, was aus der Bedeutung des Wortes tanzen nolávoa hervorgeht." Preuss, "Der Ursprung der Religion und Kunst," *Globus*, Vol. 87 (1905), p. 336.

[15] E. Reclus, *Le primitif d'Australie*, p. 28.

[16] Cf. Preuss, *Religion und Mythologie der Uitoto* (Göttingen and Leipzig, 1923), I, 123ff.; II, 637f.

be posited by language in spite of all distinctions and even complete disparity of appearances, as long as the contents of experience agree in their functional import—in this case, their religious significance.[17]

Here is one of the basic motives by virtue of which mythical thinking transcends the original vagueness of "complex" intuitions and proceeds to concretely defined, distinctly sundered, and individualized mental constructions. This process, too, is determined primarily by the lines which activity takes; so much so that the forms of mythical invention reflect, not the objective character of *things*, but the forms of human practices. The primitive god, like primitive action, is limited to a very restricted sphere. Not only does every occupation have its particular god, but each phase of the total action becomes the domain of an independent god or daemon who governs this precise sphere of action. The Roman *Fratres Arvales*, when making atonement for the removal of trees from the sacred grove of the goddess Dia, divided the deed into a number of separate acts, for each of which a special deity was invoked: *Deferenda* for fetching down the wood, *Commolenda* for chopping it up, *Coinquenda* for splitting it, and *Adolenda* for burn-

[17] Here we may adduce a further striking example of this "teleological" construction of language, which I owe to a verbal communication from my colleague Professor Otto Dempwolff. In the Kâte language, which is current in New Guinea, there is a word *bilin*, which denotes a certain kind of grass with tough stems and roots that are wedged firmly in the soil; the latter are said to hold the earth together during earthquakes, so that it does not break apart. When nails were first introduced by Europeans, and when their use became popularly known, the natives applied this word to them—as also to wire and to iron rods, in short, to everything that served the purpose of holding things together.

Similarly, one may often observe in nursery language the creation of such teleological identities, which do not meet our class concepts at all, and seem even to defy them. Cf. Clara and William Stern, *Die Kindersprache* (Leipzig, 1905), pp. 26, 172, *et al.*

ing up the brushwood.[18] The same phenomenon may be
seen in primitive languages, which often divide an action
into several subactions, and instead of comprehending
it all under one term, denote each part by a separate
verb, as though they had to break up the idea into little
pieces in order to handle it. Perhaps it is not mere chance
that in the language of the Evé, who have such a wealth
of "momentary gods" and "special gods," this peculiarity
should be very pronounced.[19] And even where both
language and myth have risen considerably above such
momentary, sense-bound intuition, where they have
broken through their original fetters, they long remain
quite inseparably involved with each other. Their connection is, in fact, so close that it is impossible to determine on a basis of empirical data which of them takes
the lead in their progress toward universal formulation
and conception, and which one merely follows suit.
Usener, in a section of his work that is philosophically
one of the most significant parts, has sought to prove
that all general terms in language have had to go through
a certain mythical phase. The fact that in the Indo-
Germanic languages abstract concepts are usually denoted by feminine nouns, with the feminine ending -a
(-η), proves, according to Usener, that the idea this
feminine form expresses was originally not conceived as
an abstractum, but apprehended and felt as a female
deity.

"Can there be any doubt," he asks further, "whether
Φόβος came first, or φόβος, the divine image or the condition? Why should the condition be denoted as something of masculine gender, not as neuter, like τὸ δέος?
The first creation of the word must have been inspired

[18] Wissowa, *Religion und Kultus der Römer*, Vol. 2, p. 25.
[19] Westermann, *Grammatik der Ewe-Sprache* (Berlin, 1907), p. 95.

by some idea of a living, personal Being, the "Startler," the "Flight Producer"; in countless applications of the supposed abstract word, this Being still appears: εἰσῆλθεν or ἐνέπεσε Φόβος, the Startler stalks, or attacks, me! The same process must be assumed for the making of all feminized abstractions. The feminine adjective only became an abstraction after it had denoted a female personage, and in primitive times this could not have been conceived as anything but a goddess" (p. 375).

But does not the science of language as well as that of religion show signs of a converse process as well? Should we not suppose, for instance, that the way which inflected languages have of endowing every noun with a particular gender may have influenced the conceptions of mythico-religious imagination and bent them after its own fashion? Or may we deem it mere chance that among peoples whose language does not differentiate genders, but employs other and more complex principles of classification, the realm of myth and religion also exhibits an entirely different structure—that it represents all phases of existence not under the auspices of personal, divine powers, but orders it according to totemic groups and classes? We shall content ourselves with merely proposing this question, which would have to be answered by detailed scientific research. But whatever the verdict might be, it is evident that myth and language play similar roles in the evolution of thought from momentary experience to enduring conceptions, from sense impression to formulation, and that their respective functions are mutually conditioned. Together and in combination they prepare the soil for the great syntheses from which our mental creation, our unified vision of the cosmos springs.

✍ 4 ⁊

Word Magic

SO far we have sought to discover the common root of linguistic and mythic conception; now arises the question, how this relationship is reflected in the structure of the "world" that is given by speech and by myth. Here we encounter a law that holds equally for all symbolic forms, and bears essentially on their evolution. None of them arise initially as separate, independently recognizable forms, but every one of them must first be emancipated from the common matrix of myth. All mental contents, no matter how truly they evince a separate systematic realm and a "principle" of their own, are actually known to us only as thus involved and grounded. Theoretical, practical and aesthetic consciousness, the world of language and of morality, the basic forms of the community and the state—they are all originally tied up with mythico-religious conceptions. This connection is so strong that where it begins to dissolve the whole intellectual world seems threatened with disruption and collapse; so vital that as the separate forms emerge from the original whole and henceforth show specific characteristics against its undifferentiated background they seem to uproot themselves and lose some of their own proper nature. Only gradually do they show that this self-imposition is part of their self-development, that the negation contains the embyro of a new assertion, that the very divorcement becomes the starting point of a new connection, which arises from extraneous postulations.

The original bond between the linguistic and the

mythico-religious consciousness is primarily expressed in
the fact that all verbal structures appear as *also* mythical
entities, endowed with certain mythical powers, that the
Word, in fact, becomes a sort of primary force, in which
all being and doing originate. In all mythical cosmog-
onies, as far back as they can be traced, this supreme
position of the Word is found. Among the texts which
Preuss has collected among the Uitoto Indians there is
one which he has adduced as a direct parallel to the opening passage of St. John, and which, in his translation,
certainly seems to fall in with it perfectly: "In the beginning," it says, "the Word gave the Father his
origin."[20] Of course, striking though it may be, no one
would try to argue from this coincidence to any direct
relationship or even an analogy of material content between that primitive creation story and the speculations
of St. John. And yet it presents us with a certain problem, it points to the fact that some indirect relationship
must obtain, which covers everything from the most
primitive gropings of mythico-religious thought to those
highest products in which such thought seems to have
already gone over into a realm of pure speculation.

A more precise insight into the foundations of this
relationship can be attained only in so far as we are able
to carry back the study of those examples of Word
veneration, which the history of religions is always un-
covering, from the mere analogy of their respective
contents to the recognition of their common *form*. There
must be some particular, essentially unchanging *function*
that endows the Word with this extraordinary, religious
character, and exalts it *ab initio* to the religious sphere,
the sphere of the "holy." In the creation accounts of
almost all great cultural religions, the Word appears in

[20] Preuss, *Religion und Mythologie der Uitoto*, I, 25 f.; II, 659.

league with the highest Lord of creation; either as the
tool which he employs or actually as the primary source
from which he, like all other Being and order of Being,
is derived. Thought and its verbal utterance are usually
taken directly as one; for the mind that thinks and the
tongue that speaks belong essentially together. Thus, in
one of the earliest records of Egyptian theology, this
primary force of "the heart and the tongue" is attributed
to the creation-god Ptah, whereby he produces and
governs all gods and men, all animals, and all that lives.
Whatever is has come into being through the thought
of his heart and the command of his tongue; to these
two, all physical and spiritual being, the existence of the
Ka as well as all properties of things, owe their origin.
Here, as indeed certain scholars have pointed out, thou-
sands of years before the Christian era, God is conceived
as a spiritual Being who *thought* the world before he
created it, and who used the Word as a means of expression and an instrument of creation.[21] And as all

[21] See Moret, *Mystères Egyptiens* (Paris, 1913), pp. 118ff., 138. Cf.
esp. Erman, "Ein Denkmal memphitischer Theologie," *Sitzungsbericht
der königlich-Preussischen Akademie der Wissenschaften*, XLIII
(1911), 916ff. An exact parallel to this may be found in a creation
hymn of Polynesia, which, according to Bastian's German translation
(here rendered into English), reads as follows:

> In the beginning, Space and the Companion,
> Space in the height of Heaven,
> Tananaoa filled; he ruled the Heaven,
> And Mutuhei wound himself above it.
> In those days was no voice, no sound,
> No living thing yet in motion.
> No day there was as yet, no light,
> Only a gloomy, black-dark night.
> Tananaoa it was who conquered the night,
> And Mutuhei's spirit the distance pierced.
> From Tananaoa Atea was sprung,
> Mighty, filled with the power of life,
> Atea it was, who now ruled the Day,
> And drove away Tananaoa."

"The basic idea is that Tananaoa induces the process in that the original physical and psychical Being rest in him, so do all ethical bonds and the whole moral order.

Those religions which base their world picture and their cosmogony essentially on a fundamental ethical contrast, the dualism of good and evil, venerate the spoken Word as the primary force by whose sole agency Chaos was transformed into an ethico-religious Cosmos. According to the Bundahish, the cosmogony and cosmography of the Parsis, the war between the power of Good and the power of Evil, i.e., between Ahura Mazda and Angra Mainyu, begins with Ahura Mazda's reciting the words of the Holy Prayer (Ahuna Vairya):

"He spake that which has twenty-one words. The end, which is his victory, the impotence of Angra Mainyu, the decline of the Daevas, the resurrection and the future life, the ending of opposition to the (good) creation for all eternity—all these he showed to Angra Mainyu . . . When a third of this prayer had been spoken, Angra Mainyu doubled up his body with terror, when two-thirds had been spoken he fell upon his knees, and when the whole had been uttered he was confounded, and powerless to abuse the creatures of Ahura Mazda, and remained confounded for three thousand years."[22]

Here, again the words of the prayer precede the material creation, and preserve it ever against the destructive powers of the Evil One. Similarly, in India, we find the

---

silence (Mutuhei) is removed through the production of Tone (Ono), and Atea (Light) is wedded with the Red Dawn (Atanua)." See Bastian, *Die heilige Sage der Polynesier, Kosmogonie u. Theologie* (Leipzig, 1881), pp. 13f; also Achelis, "Ueber Mythologie u. Kultus von Hawaii, *Das Ausland,* Vol. 66 (1893), p. 436.

[22] See *Der Bundehesh, zum ersten Male herausgegeben von Ferdinand Justi* (Leipzig, 1868), Chap. 1, p. 3.

power of the Spoken Word (Vāc) exalted even above the might of the gods themselves.

"On the Spoken Word all the gods depend, all beasts and men; in the Word live all creatures . . . the Word is the Imperishable, the firstborn of the eternal Law, the mother of the Veddas, the navel of the divine world."[23]

As the Word is first in origin, it is also supreme in power. Often it is the *name* of the deity, rather than the god himself, that seems to be the real source of efficacy.[24] Knowledge of the name gives him who knows it mastery even over the being and will of the god. Thus a familiar Egyptian legend tells how Isis, the great sorceress, craftily persuaded the sun-god Ra to disclose his name to her, and how through possession of the name she gained power over him and over all the other gods.[25] In many other ways, too, Egyptian religious life in all its phases evinces over and over again this belief in the supremacy of the name and the magic power that dwells

[23] *Taittiriya Brahm.*, 2, 8, 8, 4 (German by Gelder in his *Religionsgeschichtliches Lesebuch*, p. 125).

[24] According to the tradition of the Maori, upon their first immigration in New Zealand they did not take along their old gods, but only their mighty prayers, by means of which they were assured the power of bending the gods to their will. Cf. Brinton, *Religions of Primitive Peoples*, pp. 103f.

[25] "I am he," says Re in this story, "with many names and many shapes, and my form is in every god. . . . My father and my mother have told me my name, and it has remained hidden in my body since my birth, lest some sorcerer should acquire magic power over me thereby." Then said Isis to Re (who has been stung by a poisonous serpent of her creation, and is appealing to all the gods for help from the poison): "Tell me your name, father of gods, . . . that the poison may go out of you; for the man whose name is spoken, he lives." And the poison burned hotter than fire, so that the god could no longer resist. He said to Isis: "My name shall go forth from my body and over into thine." And he added: "Thou shalt conceal it, but to thy son Horus thou mayst reveal it as a potent spell against every poison." See Erman, *Aegypten u. aegyptisches Leben im Altertum*, II, 360ff.; *Die aegyptische Religion*, Vol. 2, pp. 173f.

in it.[26] The ceremonies attending the anointment of kings are governed by minute prescriptions for the transference of the god's several names to the Pharaoh; each name conveys a special attribute, a new divine power.[27]

Moreover, this motive plays a decisive role in the Egyptian doctrines of the soul and its immortality. The souls of the departed, starting on their journey to the land of the dead, must be given not only their physical possessions, such as food and clothing, but also a certain outfit of a magical nature: this consists chiefly of the names of the gatekeepers in the nether world, for only the knowledge of these names can unlock the doors of Death's kingdom. Even the boat in which the dead man is conveyed, and its several parts, the rudder, the mast, etc., demand that he call them by their right names; only by virtue of this appellation can he render them willing and subservient and cause them to take him to his destination.[28]

The essential identity between the word and what it denotes becomes even more patently evident if we look at it not from the objective standpoint, but from a subjective angle. For even a person's ego, his very self and personality, is indissolubly linked, in mythic thinking,

[26] Cf. the examples cited by Budge, *Egyptian Magic* (London, 1911) Vol. 2, pp. 157ff.; also Hopfner, *Griechisch-Aegyptischer Offenbarun* zauber (Leipzig, 1921), pp. 68off.

[27] Cf. esp. G. Foucart, *Histoire des religions et méthode* parative (Paris, 1912), pp. 202f.: "Donner au Pharaon un nouveau, dans lequel entrait la désignation d'un attribut ou d'une festation de l'Epervier, puis, plus tard, de Râ et l'ajouter au noms du protocol royale, c'était pour les Égyptiens introduire da royale, et superposer aux autres éléments qui la compos nveau, exceptionnel, qui était une incarnation de Râ ait bel et bien détacher de Râ une des vib chacune est lui tout entier; et en la f c'était transformer toute celle-ci matériel de la divinité."
cit., pp. 164ff.

with his name. Here the name is never a mere symbol, but is part of the personal property of its bearer; property which must be carefully protected, and the use of which is exclusively and jealously reserved to him. Sometimes it is not only his name, but also some other verbal denotation, that is thus treated as a physical possession, and as such may be acquired and usurped by someone else. Georg von der Gabelentz, in his book on the science of language, mentions the edict of a Chinese emperor of the third century B.C., whereby a pronoun in the first person, that had been legitimately in popular use, was henceforth reserved to him alone.[29] And the name may even acquire a status above the more or less accessory one of a personal possession, when it is taken as a truly substantial Being, an integral part of its bearer. As such it is in the same category as his body or his soul. It is said of the Eskimos that for them man consists of three ˈements—body, soul, and name.[30] And in Egypt, too,

‾nd a similar conception, for there the physical body

‾ was thought to be accompanied, on the one

his Ka, or double, and, on the other, by his

‾rt of spiritual double. And of all these three

just the last-mentioned which becomes

‾he expression of a man's "self," of his

‾ in far more advanced cultures this

‾ame and personality continues to

‾ law, the concept of the "legal

‾ulated, and this status was de-

‾ubjects, those subjects were

‾n of a proper name. U

‾om‾
‾nom‾
‾mani-
‾autres
‾s la per-
‾ient déjà,
‾. Ou, plus
‾ations, une
‾isant entrer
‾en un nouvel

‾e Peoples
‾lso

in it.[26] The ceremonies attending the anointment of kings are governed by minute prescriptions for the transference of the god's several names to the Pharaoh; each name conveys a special attribute, a new divine power.[27]

Moreover, this motive plays a decisive role in the Egyptian doctrines of the soul and its immortality. The souls of the departed, starting on their journey to the land of the dead, must be given not only their physical possessions, such as food and clothing, but also a certain outfit of a magical nature: this consists chiefly of the names of the gatekeepers in the nether world, for only the knowledge of these names can unlock the doors of Death's kingdom. Even the boat in which the dead man is conveyed, and its several parts, the rudder, the mast, etc., demand that he call them by their right names; only by virtue of this appellation can he render them willing and subservient and cause them to take him to his destination.[28]

The essential identity between the word and what it denotes becomes even more patently evident if we look at it not from the objective standpoint, but from a subjective angle. For even a person's ego, his very self and personality, is indissolubly linked, in mythic thinking,

[26] Cf. the examples cited by Budge, *Egyptian Magic* (London, 1911), Vol. 2, pp. 157ff.; also Hopfner, *Griechisch-Aegyptischer Offenbarungszauber* (Leipzig, 1921), pp. 680ff.

[27] Cf. esp. G. Foucart, *Histoire des religions et méthode comparative* (Paris, 1912), pp. 202f.: "Donner au Pharaon un 'nom' nouveau, dans lequel entrait la désignation d'un attribut ou d'une manifestation de l'Epervier, puis, plus tard, de Râ et l'ajouter aux autres noms du protocol royale, c'était pour les Égyptiens introduire dans la personne royale, et superposer aux autres éléments qui la composaient déjà, un être nouveau, exceptionnel, qui était une incarnation de Râ. Ou, plus exactement, c'était bel et bien détacher de Râ une des vibrations, une des âmes forces, dont chacune est lui tout entier; et en la faisant entrer dans la personne du Roi, c'était transformer toute celle-ci en un nouvel exemplaire, un nouveau support matériel de la divinité."

[28] For further details see Budge, *op. cit.*, pp. 164ff.

with his name. Here the name is never a mere symbol, but is part of the personal property of its bearer; property which must be carefully protected, and the use of which is exclusively and jealously reserved to him. Sometimes it is not only his name, but also some other verbal denotation, that is thus treated as a physical possession, and as such may be acquired and usurped by someone else. Georg von der Gabelentz, in his book on the science of language, mentions the edict of a Chinese emperor of the third century B.C., whereby a pronoun in the first person, that had been legitimately in popular use, was henceforth reserved to him alone.[29] And the name may even acquire a status above the more or less accessory one of a personal possession, when it is taken as a truly substantial Being, an integral part of its bearer. As such it is in the same category as his body or his soul. It is said of the Eskimos that for them man consists of three elements—body, soul, and name.[30] And in Egypt, too, we find a similar conception, for there the physical body of man was thought to be accompanied, on the one hand, by his Ka, or double, and, on the other, by his name, as a sort of spiritual double. And of all these three elements it is just the last-mentioned which becomes more and more the expression of a man's "self," of his "personality."[31] Even in far more advanced cultures this connection between name and personality continues to be felt. When, in Roman law, the concept of the "legal person" was formally articulated, and this status was denied to certain physical subjects, those subjects were also denied official possession of a proper name. Under

[29] *Die Sprachwissenschaft*, p. 228.
[30] See Brinton, *Religions of Primitive Peoples*, p. 93.
[31] Cf. Budge, op. cit., p. 157; also Moret, *Mystères Egyptiens*, p. 119.

Roman law a slave had no legal name, because he could not function as a legal person.[32]

In other ways, too, the unity and uniqueness of the name is not only a mark of the unity and uniqueness of the person, but actually constitutes it; the name is what first makes man an individual. Where this verbal distinctiveness is not found, there the outlines of his personality tend also to be effaced. Among the Algonquins, a man who bears the same name as some given person is regarded as the latter's other self, his alter ego.[33] If, in accordance with a prevalent custom, a child is given the name of his grandfather, this expresses the belief that the grandfather is resurrected, reincarnated in the boy. As soon as a child is born, the problem arises which one of his departed ancestors is reborn in him; only after this has been determined by the priest can the ceremony be performed whereby the infant receives that progenitor's name.[34]

Furthermore, the mythic consciousness does not see human personality as something fixed and unchanging, but conceives every phase of a man's life as a new personality, a new self; and this metamorphosis is first of all made manifest in the changes which his name undergoes. At puberty a boy receives a new name, because, by virtue of the magical rites accompanying his initiation, he has ceased to exist as a boy, and has been reborn as a

[32] Mommsen, *Römisches Staatsrecht*, III, 1, p. 203; cf. Rudolph Hirzel, "Der Name—ein Beitrag zu seiner Geschichte im Altertum u. besonders bei den Griechen," *Abhandlungen der sächsischen Gesellschaft der Wissenschaften*, Vol. XXVI (1918), p. 10.

[33] "The expression in the Algonkin tongue for a person of the same name is *nind owiawina*, 'He is another myself.'" (Cuoq, *Lexique Algonquine*, p. 113, quoted from Brinton, *op. cit.*, p. 93). Cf. esp. Giesebrecht, *Die alttestamentliche Schätzung des Gottesnamens in ihrer religionsgeschichtlichen Grundlage* (Königsberg, 1901), p. 89.

[34] See, for instance, Spieth, *Die Religion der Eweer*, p. 229.

man, the reincarnation of one of his ancestors.[35] In other
cases the change of name sometimes serves to protect a
man against impending danger; he escapes by taking on
a different self, whose form makes him unrecognizable.
Among the Evé it is customary to give children, and
especially those whose elder brothers or sisters have died
young, a name that has a frightful connotation, or attributes some non-human nature to them; the idea is
that Death may be either frightened away, or deceived,
and will pass them by as though they were not human
at all.[36] Similarly, the name of a man laboring under disease or bloodguilt is sometimes changed, on the same
principle, that Death may not find him. Even in Greek
culture this custom of altering names, with its mythic
motivation, still maintained itself.[37] Quite generally, in
fact, the being and life of a person is so intimately connected with his name that, as long as the name is pre-
served and spoken, its bearer is still felt to be present and
directly active. The dead may, at any moment, be literally "invoked," the moment those who survive him speak
his name. As everyone knows, the fear of such visitation
has led many savages to avoid not only every mention
of the departed, whose name is tabooed, but even the
enunciation of all assonances to his name. Often, for
instance, an animal species whose name a defunct person
had borne has to be given a different appellation, lest
the dead man be inadvertently called upon by speaking

[35] Characteristic examples may be found especially among the initia-
tion rites of Australian native tribes; cf. esp. Howitt, *The Native
Tribes of South East Australia* (London, 1904), and James, *Primitive
Ritual and Belief* (London, 1917), pp. 16 ff.

[36] Cf. Spieth, *op. cit.*, p. 230.
[37] Hermippos 26, 7:

διὰ τοῦτο καλῶς ἡμῖν θεῖοι καὶ ἱεροὶ ἄνδρες ἐθέσπισαν ἐναλλάττειν τὰ τῶν
ἀποιχομένων ὀνόματα, ὅπως τελωνοῦντας αὐτοὺς κατὰ τὸν ἐναέριον τόπον
λανθάνειν ἐξῇ καὶ διέρχεσθαι.

of the beast.[38] In many cases procedures of this sort, entirely mythic in their motivation, have had a radical influence on language, and modified vocabularies considerably.[39] And the further a Being's power extends, the more mythic potency and "significance" he embodies, the greater is the sphere of influence of his name. The rule of secrecy, therefore, applies first and foremost to the Holy Name; for the mention of it would immediately release all the powers inherent in the god himself.[40]

Here, again, we are faced with one of the prime and essential motives which, rooted as it is in the deepest layers of mythical thought and feeling, maintains itself even in the highest religious formulations. Giesebrecht has traced the origin, extent and development of this motive throughout the Old Testament, in his work, *Die alttestamentliche Schätzung des Gottesnamens und ihre religionsgeschichtliche Grundlage*. But early Christianity, too, still labored entirely under the spell of this idea.

"The fact that the name functions as proxy for its bearer," says Dieterich in his *Eine Mithrasliturgie*, "and to speak the name may be equal to calling a person into being; that a name is feared because it is a real power;

[38] Ten Kate, "Notes ethnographiques sur les Comanches," *Revue d'Ethnographie*, IV, 131 (cited from Preuss, "Ursprung der Religion u. Kunst," *Globus*, Vol. 87, p. 395).

[39] Name taboos, I am told in a personal communication from Meinhof, play a vital part especially in Africa; among many Bantu tribes, for instance, women are not allowed to speak the names of their husbands or their fathers, so they are compelled to invent new words.

[40] For later Greek magical practices, cf. Hopfner, *Griechisch-ägyptischer Offenbarungszauber*, § 701, p. 179: "Je höher und mächtiger der Gott war, desto kräftiger und wirksamer musste auch sein wahrer Name sein. Daher ist es ganz folgerichtig anzunehmen, dass der wahre Name des einen Urgotts, des Schöpfers (δημιουργός) für Menschen überhaupt unerträglich sei: denn dieser Name war ja zugleich auch das Göttliche an sich und zwar in seiner höchsten Potenz, daher für die schwache Natur des Sterblichen viel zu stark; daher tötet er den, der ihn hört."

that knowledge of it is sought because being able to speak it bestows control of that power on the knower—all these facts indicate clearly what the early Christians were still feeling and trying to express when they said 'In God's name' instead of 'In God,' or 'In Christ's name' for 'In Christ.' . . . Thus we can understand such expressions as βαπτίζειν εἰς τὸ ὄνομα Χριστοῦ instead of βαπτίζειν εἰς Χριστόν; the name is pronounced over the font, and thereby takes possession of the water and pervades it, so that the neophyte is quite literally immersed in the name of the Lord. The congregation, whose liturgy begins with the words: 'In the name of God,' was thought at the time to be within the bourne of the name's efficacy (no matter how figuratively and formally the phrase is taken). 'Where two or three are gathered together in my name, (εἰς τὸ ἐμὸν ὄνομα) there am I in the midst of them' (Matthew 18:20) means simply, 'Where they pronounce my name in their assembly, there I am really present.' Ἁγιασθήτω τὸ ὄνομά σου once had a much more concrete sense than one would ever suspect from the hermeneutics of the several churches and their doctrines."[41]

The "special god," too, lives and acts only in the particular domain to which his name assigns and holds him. Whoever, therefore, would be assured of his protection and aid must be sure to enter his realm, i.e., to call him by his "right" name. This need explains the phraseology of prayer, and of religious speech in general, both in Greece and in Rome—all the turns of phrase which ring a change on the several names of the god, in order to obviate the danger of missing the proper and essential appellation. Concerning the Greeks, this practice is recorded for us by a well-known passage in Plato's *Kraty-*

[41] Dieterich, *Eine Mithrasliturgie*, pp. 111, 114f.

los;[42] in Rome it produced a standing formula, in which the various terms of invocation, corresponding to the several aspects of the god's nature and will, are disjoined by "either — or," "*sive — sive.*"[43] This stereotyped mode of address must be repeated every time; for every act of devotion to the god, every appeal directed to him, commands his attention only if he is invoked by his appropriate name. The art of right address, therefore, was developed in Rome to the point of a sacerdotal technique, which produced the *indigitamenta* in the keeping of the pontifices.[44]

But here let us stop; for it is not our intention to collect theological or ethnological material, but to clarify and define the problem presented by such material. Such interweaving and interlocking as we have found between the elements of language, and the various forms of religious and mythical conception cannot be due to mere chance; it must be rooted in a common characteristic of language and myth as such. Some scholars have sought to base this intimate connection on the suggestive power of words, and especially of a spoken command, to which primitive man is supposed to be particularly subject; the magical and daemonic power which all verbal utterance has for the mythic state of consciousness seems to them to be nothing more than an objectification of that experience. But such a narrow empirical and pragmatic foundation, such a detail of personal or social experience, cannot support the prime and fundamental facts of linguistic and mythic conception. More and more clearly we see ourselves faced with the question whether the close

---

[42] Plato, *Kratylos*, 400E.

[43] For details see Norden, *Agnostos Theos: Untersuchungen zur Formengeschichte religiöser Rede* (Leipzig, 1913), pp. 143 ff.

[44] Cf. Wissowa, *Religion und Kultus der Römer*, Vol. 2, p. 37.

relationship of contents which certainly obtains between language and myth may not be most readily explained by the common form of their evolution, by the conditions which govern both verbal expression and mythic imagination from their earliest, unconscious beginnings. We have found these conditions given by a type of apprehension that is contrary to theoretical, discursive thinking. For, as the latter tends toward expansion, implication and systematic connection, the former tends toward concentration, telescoping, separate characterization. In discursive thought, the particular phenomenon is related to the whole pattern of being and of process; with ever-tightening, ever more elaborate bonds it is held to that totality. In mythic conception, however, things are not taken for what they mean indirectly, but for their immediate appearance; they are taken as pure presentations, and embodied in the imagination. It is easy to see that this sort of hypostatization must lead to an entirely different attitude toward the spoken word, toward its power and content, than the standpoint of discursive thought would produce. For theoretical thinking, a word is essentially a vehicle serving the fundamental aim of such ideation: the establishment of relationships between the given phenomenon and others which are "like" it or otherwise connected with it according to some co-ordinating law. The significance of discursive thought lies entirely in this function. In this sense, it is something essentially ideal, a "sign" or symbol, the object of which is not a substantial entity but lies rather in the relations it establishes. The word stands, so to speak, *between* actual particular impressions, as a phenomenon of a different order, a new intellectual dimension; and to this mediating position, this remoteness from the sphere of immediate data, it owes the freedom and ease with which it moves among specific objects and connects one with another.

This free ideality, which is the core of its *logical* nature, is necessarily lacking in the realm of mythic conception. For in this realm nothing has any significance or being save what is given in tangible reality. Here is no "reference" and "meaning"; every content of consciousness to which the mind is directed is immediately translated into terms of actual presence and effectiveness. Here thought does not confront its data in an attitude of free contemplation, seeking to understand their structure and their systematic connections, and analyzing them according to their parts and functions, but is simply captivated by a total impression. Such thinking does not develop the given content of experience; it does not reach backward or forward from that vantage point to find "causes" and "effects," but rests content with taking in the sheer existent. When Kant defined "reality" as any content of empirical intuition which follows general laws and thus takes its place in the "context of experience," he gave an exhaustive definition of the concept of reality in the canons of discursive thought. But mythic ideation and primitive verbal conception recognize no such "context of experience." Their function, as we have seen, is rather a process of almost violent separation and individuation. Only when this intense individuation has been consummated, when the immediate intuition has been focused and, one might say, reduced to a single point, does the mythic or linguistic form emerge, and the word or the momentary god is created. And this peculiar genesis determines the type of intellectual content that is common to language and myth; for where the process of apprehension aims not at an expansion, extension, universalizing of the content, but rather at its highest intensification, this fact cannot fail to influence human consciousness. All other things are lost to a mind thus enthralled; all bridges between the concrete datum and the systematized totality of experience are broken; only the present reality, as mythic or linguistic conception stresses and shapes it, fills the entire subjective realm. So this one content of experience must reign over practically the whole experiential world. There is nothing beside or beyond it whereby it could be measured or to which it could be compared; its mere presence is the sum of all Being. At this point, the word which denotes that thought content is not a mere conventional symbol, but is merged with its object in an indissoluble unity. The conscious experience is not merely wedded to the word, but is consumed by it. Whatever has been fixed by a name, henceforth is not only real, but is Reality. The potential between "symbol" and "meaning" is resolved; in place of a more or less adequate "expression," we find a relation of identity, of complete congruence between "image" and "object," between the name and the thing.

From another angle, too, we may observe and elucidate this substantial embodiment which the spoken word undergoes: for the same sort of hypostatization or transubstantiation occurs in other realms of mental creativity; indeed, it seems to be the typical process in all unconscious ideation. All cultural work, be it technical or purely intellectual, proceeds by the gradual shift from the direct relation between man and his environment to an indirect relation. In the beginning, sensual impulse is followed immediately by its gratification; but gradually more and more mediating terms intervene between the will and its object. It is as though the will, in order to gain its end, had to move away from the goal instead of toward it; instead of a simple reaction, almost in the nature of a reflex, to bring the object into reach, it requires a differentiation of behavior, covering a wider class of objects, so that finally the sum total of all these acts, by the use of various "means," may realize the desired end.

In the realm of technical achievement this increasing mediation may be seen in the invention and use of tools. But here, again, it may be observed that as soon as man employs a tool, he views it not as a mere artifact of which he is the recognized maker, but as a Being in its own right, endowed with powers of its own. Instead of being governed by his will, it becomes a god or daemon on whose will he depends—to which he feels himself subjected, and which he adores with the rites of a religious cult. Especially the ax and the hammer seem to have attained such religious significance in earliest times;[45] but the cult of other implements, too, such as the hoe or the fishhook, the spear or the sword, may be found to this day among primitive peoples. Among the Evé the smith's hammer (Zu) is deemed a mighty deity whom they worship and to whom they make sacrifices.[46] And even in Greek religion and Greek classical literature the sentiment that prompts such a cult often finds direct expression. As an example of this, Usener has drawn attention to a passage in the Seven against Thebes of Aeschylos, in which Parthenopaeus swears by his spear, which he "honors above god, and above his eyes," to destroy Thebes. "Life and Victory depend upon direction and power, as also on the good will of the weapon; this feeling wells up irresistibly in the crucial moment of the

[45] Examples of this may be found, e.g., in Beth's *Einführung in die vergleichende Religionsgeschichte* (Leipzig, 1920), pp. 24ff.
[46] Spieth, *Religion der Eweer*, p. 115.

battle; and prayer does not invoke a god from afar to guide the weapon—the weapon itself is god, the helper and deliverer."[47]

An implement, then, is never regarded as something simply manufactured, something thought of and produced, but as a "gift from above." Its origin does not go back to man himself, but to some "culture hero," either a god or an animal. This attribution of all cultural values to a "savior" is so universal that attempts have been made to find the essence and origin of the god concept in this notion.[48] Again we are faced with a characteristic of mythic thinking which divides it sharply from the way of "discursive," or theoretical, reflection. The latter is characterized by the fact that even in apparently immediately "given" data it recognizes an element of mental creation, and stresses this active ingredient. Even in matters of fact it reveals an aspect of mental formulation; even in sheer sense data it traces the influence of a "spontaneity of thought" that goes to their making.— But while logical reflection tends, in this wise, to resolve all receptivity into spontaneity, mythic conception shows exactly the opposite tendency, namely, to regard all spontaneous action as receptive, and all human achievement as something merely bestowed. This holds for all the technical means of culture, and no less for its intellectual tools. For between these two sorts of implement there is originally no sharp dividing line, but rather a fluid distinction. Even purely mental assets and achievements, such as the words of human speech, are at first conceived entirely in the category of physical existence and the physical support of mankind. Preuss

[47] Usener, *Götternamen*, p. 285.
[48] Cf. Kurt Breysig, *Die Entstehung des Gottesgedankens u. der Heilbringer*, Berlin, 1905.

reports that, according to the Cora Indians and the
Uitoto, the "Patriarch" created men and nature, but that
since this creation he no longer interferes directly with
the course of events. In lieu of such personal intervention, he gave to men his "Words," i.e., his cult and the
religious ceremonies by means of which they now control nature and attain whatever is necessary for the wel-
fare and perpetuation of the race. Without these holy
spells which were originally given into their keeping,
men would be entirely helpless, for nature yields nothing merely in return for human labor.[49] Among the
Cherokees, too, it is an accepted belief that success in
hunting or fishing is due chiefly to the use of certain
words, of the proper magic formulas.[50]

It was a long evolutionary course which the human
mind had to traverse, to pass from the belief in a
physico-magical power comprised in the Word to a
realization of its spiritual power. Indeed, it is the Word,
it is language, that really reveals to man that world
which is closer to him than any world of natural objects
and touches his weal and woe more directly than physical
nature. For it is language that makes his existence in a
community possible; and only in society, in relation to
a "Thee," can his subjectivity assert itself as a "Me."
But here again the creative act, while it is in progress,
is not recognized as such; all the energy of that spiritual
achievement is projected into the result of it, and seems
bound up in that object from which it seems to emanate
as by reflection. Here, too, as in the case of tools and

[49] For details see Preuss, *Die Nayarit-Expedition*, I, lxviiif.; *Religion u. Mythologie der Uitoto* I, 25f; cf. also Preuss's article: "Die höchste Gottheit bei den kulturarmen Völkern," *Psychol. Forschungen*, II, 1922.

[50] Cf. Mooney, "Sacred Formulas of the Cherokee," *VIIth Annual Report of the Bureau of Ethnology* (Smithsonian Institution).

instruments, all spontaneity is felt as receptivity, all
creativity as being, and every product of subjectivity as
so much substantiality. And yet, this very hypostatization of the Word is of crucial importance in the development of human mentality. For it is the first form in
which the spiritual power inherent in language can be
apprehended at all; the Word has to be conceived in
the mythic mode, as a substantive being and power,
before it can be comprehended as an ideal instrument,
an organon of the mind, and as a fundamental function
in the construction and development of spiritual reality.

❧ 5 ☙

The Successive Phases of Religious Thought

ACCORDING to Usener, the lowest level to which we
can trace back the origin of religious concepts is that
of "momentary gods," as he calls those images which
are born from the need or the specific feeling of a critical
moment, sprung from the excitation of mythico-religious
fantasy, and still bearing the mark of all its pristine
volatility and freedom. But it appears that the new findings which ethnology and comparative religion have put
at our disposal during the three decades since the publi-
cation of Usener's work enable us to go back one step
further yet. A few years before Usener's book there appeared a work by the English missionary Codrington:
*The Melanesians: Studies in their Anthropology and
Folk-Lore* (1891), which enriched the discipline of religious history by a very important concept. Codrington

shows the root of all Melanesian religion to be the concept of a "supernatural power," which permeates all things and events, and may be present now in objects, now in persons, yet is never bound exclusively to any single and individual subject or object as its host, but may be transmitted from place to place, from thing to thing, from person to person. In this light, the whole existence of things and the activity of mankind seem to be embedded, so to speak, in a mythical "field of force," an atmosphere of potency which permeates everything, and which may appear in concentrated form in certain extraordinary objects, removed from the realm of everyday affairs, or in specially endowed persons, such as distinguished warriors, priests, or magicians. The core of this world view, however, of the "mana" concept which Codrington found among the Melanesians, is not so much the idea of such particular embodiments, as the notion of a "power" in general, able to appear now in this form, now in that, to enter into one object and then into another; a power that is venerated for its "holiness" as well as feared for the dangers it contains. For that power which is conceived in a positive sense as "mana" has also a negative aspect as the power of "taboo." Every manifestation of the divine potency, be it vested in persons or things, animate or inanimate, falls outside the realm of the "profane," and belongs to a special sphere of being which has to be separated from the ordinary and mundane by set lines of division, and by all sorts of protective measures.

Since Codrington's early discoveries, the science of ethnology has proceeded to trace the diffusion of these concepts all over the earth. Certain terms that correspond exactly to the meaning of mana may be found not only among the South Sea Islanders, but also among a great many American Indian tribes, as well as in Australia and in Africa. Precisely the same notion of a universal, essentially undifferentiated Power may be found in the Algonquin "manitu," the "wakanda" of the Sioux, the "orenda" of the Iroquois, and in various African religions. On the basis of such observations, students of ethnology and comparative religion have largely come to regard this conception not merely as a universal *phenomenon,* but as nothing less than a special *category* of mythic consciousness. The "Taboo-Mana Formula" has been regarded as the "minimum definition of religion," i.e., as the expression of a distinction which constitutes one of the essential, indispensable conditions of religious life as such, and represents the lowest level of it that we know.[51]

Concerning the proper interpretation of this formula, and of the mana concept and its various equivalents, ethnologists have, indeed, reached no general agreement. In fact, their several renderings and attempted explanations still stand in complete variance to one another. "Preanimistic" theories alternate with "animistic" ones; interpretations which treat the mana as something material are opposed to others which stress its dynamic nature and tend to regard it purely as a force.[52] But this very disagreement may serve to bring us closer to the actual sense of the mana conception; for it demonstrates

[51] Cf. especially Marett, "The Taboo-mana Formula as a minimum Definition of Religion," *Archiv für Religionswissenschaft,* XII (1909), and "The Conception of Mana," *Transactions of the 3rd Internat. Congress for the Hist. of Religion* (Oxford, 1908), I (reprinted in *The Threshold of Religion,* London, 1909, 3rd ed. 1914, pp. 99ff). See also Hewitt, "Orenda and a Definition of Religion," *American Anthropologist,* N.S. IV (1902), pp. 36ff.

[52] An excellent critical survey of the various theories represented in ethnological literature may be found in F. R. Lehmann's work, *Mana; der Begriff des "Ausserordentlich Wirkungsvollen" bei Südseevölkern,* Leipzig, 1922.

the fact that this conception is still quite indifferent, one might say "neutral," to a host of distinctions which our theoretical view of being and happening and our advanced religious feeling would apply to it. A survey of the available material tends rather to show that this indifference is an essential trait of the mana conception, and that the more one tries to "determine" it, i.e., to interpret it in the categories of distinctions and contradictions familiar to our thinking, the more widely one misses its true nature. Codrington himself attempted the first and most obvious characterization of it when he described it as not only a supernatural and magical power, but a mental or "spiritual" power as well. But the problematical aspect of this characterization appeared even in his own examples of it. For they show clearly that the content and compass of the mana idea do not coincide at all with our idea of the "spiritual"—whether the latter be conceived as something of *personal* character, or merely as determined by an *animate*, as opposed to inanimate, nature.[53] For not everything animate, nor everything spiritual possesses mana, but only that which, for one reason or another, is endowed with heightened, extraordinary effective powers; and moreover, mana may belong to mere things, if they exhibit some rare form that excites the mythic imagination, and thereby rise above the realm of everyday experience. It appears, therefore, that the idea of mana and the various conceptions related to it are not bound to a particular realm of *objects* (animate or inanimate, physical or spiritual), but that they should rather be said to indicate a certain "character," which may be attributed to the most diverse objects and

[53] Hewitt demonstrates, through a detailed linguistic comparison, that the *orenda* of the Iroquois, too, is not equivalent to their notions of either spiritual forces or merely life forces, but is a conception and expression *sui generis* (*op. cit.*, p. 44 ff.).

events, if only these evoke mythic "wonder" and stand
forth from the ordinary background of familiar, mundane existence. As Söderblom says, in summarizing the
results of his exhaustive and exact analysis of the concept: "The words in question [mana, manitu, orenda,
etc.] have ambivalent meaning and are variously translated as remarkable, very strong, very great, very old,
strong in magic, wise in magic, supernatural, divine—
or in a substantive sense as power, magic, sorcery, for-
tune, success, godhead, delight."[54]

Such meanings, utterly disparate to our logical sense,
can yield some sort of unity only if this unity be sought
in a certain type not of content, but of mental attitude,
of conception. It is not a matter of "what," but of "how";
not the object of attention, but the sort of attention
directed to it, is the crucial factor here. Mana and its
several equivalents do not denote a single, definite predicate; but in all of them we find a peculiar and consistent
form of predication. This predication may indeed be
designated as the primeval mythico-religious predication,
since it expresses the spiritual "crisis" whereby the holy
is divided from the profane, and set apart from the
sphere of the ordinary, in a religious sense indifferent,
reality. By this process of division the object of religious
experience may really be said to be brought into existence,
and the realm in which it moves to be first established.
And herewith we have arrived at the crucial factor for
our general problem: for our original aim was to treat
both language and myth as spiritual functions which do
not take their departure from a world of given objects,
divided according to fixed and finished "attributes," but
which actually first produce this organization of reality

[54] Söderblom, *Das Werden des Gottesglaubens; Untersuchungen über die Anfänge der Religion* (German ed., Leipzig, 1916), p. 95.

and make the positing of attributes possible. The concept of mana and the correlative, negative concept of taboo reveal the ways in which this construction is originally effected.

From the fact that we are here moving on a level where the mythic and religious world has not yet attained any fixed form, but is presented to us, so to speak, *in statu nascendi,* we may gain insight into the many-colored, variegated play of meanings in the word—and the concept—of mana. It is quite telling that even the attempt to determine the word class to which it belongs seems to encounter difficulties at every turn. According to our habits of thinking and speaking, the easiest way is to take it simply as a noun. This makes mana a sort of substance, which represents the quintessence of all the magic powers contained in individual things. It creates a unified existent thing, which may, however, distribute itself over various beings or objects. And since, moreover, this unity was conceived not only as existent, but as animate and personified, the concept of mana was endowed with our own basic notion of "spirit"—witness the way one has often interpreted the manitu of the Algonquins and the wakanda of the Sioux as nothing but their respective designations of the "Great Spirit," which, one naturally assumed, they adored as the creator of the world.

But a more precise analysis of the words and their meanings has nowhere borne out this interpretation. It showed that quite apart from any category of *personal* being, which is never really strictly applicable, even the mere concept of a thing with independent, substantial existence is too rigid to render the fleeting, elusive idea that is here to be grasped. Thus McGee observed, concerning the wakanda of the Sioux, that the reports of missionaries, according to which it expressed the concept of a personal, original being, were completely discredited by more scholarly language studies. "Among these tribes the creation and control of the world and the things thereof are ascribed to 'wa-ka^n-da' (the term varying somewhat from tribe to tribe), just as among the Algonquin tribes omnipotence was ascribed to 'mani-do' ('Manito the Mighty' of 'Hiawatha'); yet inquiry shows that waka^{n}da assumes various forms, and is rather a quality than a definite entity. Thus among many of the tribes the sun is waka^{n}da—not *the* waka^{n}da or a waka^{n}da, but simply waka^{n}da; and among the same tribes the moon is waka^{n}da, and so is thunder, lightning, the stars, the winds, the cedar, and various other things; even a man, especially a shaman, might be waka^{n}da or a waka^{n}da. In addition the term was applied to mythic monsters of the earth, air, and waters; and according to some of the sages the ground or earth, the mythic underworld, the ideal upperworld, darkness, etc., were waka^{n}da or waka^{n}das. So, too, the fetiches and the ceremonial objects and decorations. . . . In like manner many natural objects and places of striking character were considered waka^{n}da. Thus the term was applied to all sorts of entities and ideas, and was used (with or without inflectional variations) indiscriminately as substantive and adjective, and with slight modification as verb and adverb. Manifestly a term so protean is not susceptible of translation into the more highly differentiated language of civilization. Manifestly, too, the idea expressed by the term is indefinite, and cannot justly be rendered into 'spirit,' much less 'Great Spirit'; though it is easy to understand how the superficial inquirer, dominated by definite spiritual concept(s), handicapped by unfamiliarity with the Indian tongue, misled by ignorance of the vague prescriptorial ideation, and perhaps deceived by crafty native informants or mischievous interpreters, came to adopt and perpetuate the erroneous interpretation. The term may be translated into 'mystery' perhaps more satisfactorily than into any other single English word, yet this rendering is at the same time much too limited and much too definite. As used by the Siouan Indian, waka^{n}da vaguely connotes also 'power,' 'sacred,' 'ancient,' 'grandeur,' 'animate,' 'immortal,' and other words, yet does not express with any degree of fullness and clearness the ideas conveyed by these terms singly or collectively—indeed, no English sentence of reasonable length can do justice to the aboriginal idea expressed by the term waka^{n}da."[55]

According to the findings of ethnologists and philologists, much the same thing is true of the Divine Name in the Bantu languages, and of the fundamental intuition it embodies. These tongues offer a special criterion whereby we may evaluate the conception in question; for the Bantu languages divide all nouns into different classes, and as they draw a sharp distinction between personal and impersonal nouns, the subsumption of the Divine Name under one of these heads allows us to infer immediately the character it denotes. And as a matter of fact the word *mulungu*, which our missionaries have accepted as the equivalent of our word "God," is assigned in the East Bantu dialect, for instance, to the impersonal class of nouns, to which its prefix and other formal characteristics assimilate it. Of course, this fact in itself still allows of other interpretation; it is possible to view such linguistic properties as signs of degeneration, indicating a regress of religious consciousness.

---

[55] McGee, "The Siouan Indians," *15th annual report of the Bureau of Ethnology* (Smithsonian Institution), pp. 128f.

Roehl, for instance, says in his grammar of the Shambala language:

"The conception of God as a personal being has been practically lost among the Shambalas; they speak of God as of an impersonal spirit, inherent in all nature. The *Mulungu* lives in the bush, in separate trees, in cliffs, in caves, in wild animals (lions, snakes, cats), in birds, in locusts, etc. For such a *Mulungu* there is no possible place in class I (the personal class)."[56]

An exactly opposite interpretation has been given by Meinhof, who summarizes the results of a painstaking analysis of the mulungu concept in the light of religious and linguistic studies, to the effect that the word denotes primarily the *place* of ancestral spirits and, secondly, the *power* which emanates from that spot. "But this power remains something ghostly; it is not personified, and accordingly is not treated grammatically as a personal entity, except where a foreign religion has introduced a heightened conception of its nature."[57] Examples of this

---

[56] Roehl, *Versuch einer systematischen Grammatik der Schambala-sprache* (Hamburg, 1911), pp. 45ff. Another characteristic report on the "impersonal" nature of the mulungu concept is contained in Hetherwick's account of its use among the Yao of British Central Africa: "In its native use and form the word [mulungu] does not imply personality, for it does not belong to the personal class of nouns. . . . Its form denotes rather a state or property inhering in something, as the life or health inheres in body. Among the various tribes where the word is in use as we have described, the missionaries have adopted it as the word for 'God.' But the untaught Yao refuses to assign to it any idea of being a personality. It is to him more a quality or faculty of the human nature whose signification he has extended so as to embrace the whole spirit world. Once after I have endeavored to impress an old Yao headman with the personality of the Godhead in the Christian sense of the term, using the term *Mulungu*, my listener began to talk of 'Che Mulungu,' 'Mr. God,' showing that originally to him the word conveyed no idea of the personality I was ascribing to it." Hetherwick, "Some animistic beliefs among the Yaos of British Central Africa," *Journal of the Anthropol. Inst. of Great Britain and Ireland*, XXXII (1902), p. 94.

[57] Meinhof, "Die Gottesvorstellung bei den Bantu," *Allgemeine Missions-Zeitschrift*, Vol. 50 (1923), p. 69.

sort are instructive for us especially because they show us that the level of mythic conception on which we find ourselves here corresponds to a level of linguistic conception to which we may not assign offhand our grammatical categories, our neat classifications of sharply distinguished words. If we would have a verbal analogue to the mythic conceptions here at issue, we must, apparently, go back to the most primitive level of *interjections*.[58] The manitu of the Algonquins, the mulungu of the Bantus is used in this way—as an exclamation which indicates not so much a thing as a certain *impression*, and which is used to greet anything unusual, wonderful, marvelous or terrifying.[59]

At this point one can see how far prior the level of consciousness which begets these verbal forms is even to that on which the "momentary gods" are produced. For the momentary god, despite his transiency, is nevertheless always an individual, personal form, whereas here the holy, the divine, that which besets a man with sudden terror or wonder, still has an entirely impersonal, one might say "anonymous," character. But this nameless Presence forms the background against which definite daemonic or divine images can take shape. If the "mo-

[58] In a few cases this connection may still be traced even etymologically. Thus Brinton derives the wakanda of the Sioux from an interjection of wonder and amazement (*Religions of Primitive Peoples,* p. 60).

[59] According to a report by Roger Williams, cited by Söderblom (*op. cit.,* p. 100), it is customary among the Algonquins, when they note anything unusual in men, women, birds, beasts, or fish, to exclaim: *Manitu!* that is: "This is a god!" When therefore, they converse with each other of English ships and great buildings, of plowing the fields, and especially of books and letters, they end with: "*Mannitowok,*" "Those are gods," "*Cummannitowok,*" "You are a god." Compare especially Hetherwick, *op. cit.,* p. 94: "*Mulungu* is regarded as the agent in anything mysterious. It's *mulungu,* is the Yao exclamation on being shown anything that is beyond the range of his understanding. The rainbow is always 'mulungu' although some Yaos have begun to use the Mang' anya term 'uta wa Lesa,' 'bow of Lesa.'"

mentary god" is the first *actual* form originated by the creative, mythico-religious consciousness, this actuality is grounded, none the less, in the general potency of mythico-religious feeling.[60] The division of the realm of the "holy" from that of the "profane" is the prerequisite for any *definite* divinities whatsoever. The Self feels steeped, as it were, in a mythico-religious atmosphere, which ever enfolds it, and in which it now lives and moves; it takes only a spark, a touch, to create the god or daemon out of this charged atmosphere. The outlines of such daemonic beings may be ever so vague—yet they indicate the first step in a new direction.[61]

At this point, mythic thinking veers from its original, "anonymous" stage to the exact opposite, the phase of "polynomy." Every deity unites in itself a wealth of attributes, which originally belonged to the special gods that have all been combined in one new god. Their successor, however, inherits not only all their attributes, but also their names—not as his proper name, but as appellatives; for the name and nature of the god are the same thing. Thus the polynomy of the personal deities is an essential trait in their very being. "For religious feeling,

[60] This expression of "potency" has been involuntarily adopted by those who have sought to describe the mana conception and its related notions; cf., e.g., Hewitt's definition (op. cit., p. 38): "Orenda is a hypothetic potency or potentiality to do or effect results mystically." Cf. also Hartland's Presidential Address in the *Report of the British Association for the Advancement of Science*, York, 1906, pp. 678 ff.

[61] Again, symptoms of this "indeterminateness" may be found in language, in the ways such daemonic natures are frequently denoted; for instance, in the Bantu dialects the names of such beings do not have the prefix of the first class, which comprises names of "independent agents, persons"; there is, instead, a separate prefix, which, according to Meinhof, is used for spirits, in so far as they are regarded "not as independent personalities, but as that which animates or befalls persons; thus they apply to sicknesses, as also to smoke, fire, streams, or the moon, as natural powers." (Meinhof, *Grundzüge einer vergleichenden Grammatik der Bantusprachen*, Berlin, 1906, pp. 6f. Cf. note 59.)

the power of a god is expressed in the abundance of his epithets; polynomy is a prerequisite for a god of the higher, personal order."[62] In the Egyptian writings, Isis appears as the thousand-named, the ten-thousand-named, the myrionyma;[63] in the Koran, Allah's might finds expression in his "hundred names." In the native American religions, too, and especially the Mexican, this wealth of divine names is illustrated.[64]

So it may be said that the concept of godhead really receives its first concrete development and richness through language. As it emerges into the bright light of speech, it ceases thereby to be a mere outline and a shade. But a contrary impulse, too, inherent in the nature of language, is awakened anew in this process: for as speech has a tendency to divide, determine and fixate, so it has also, no less strongly, a tendency to generalize. So, guided by language, the mythic mind finally reaches a point where it is no longer contented with the variety, abundance and concrete fullness of divine attributes and names, but where it seeks to attain, through the unity of the word, the unity of the God-idea. But even here man's mind does not rest content; beyond this unity, it strives for a concept of Being that is unlimited by any particular manifestation, and therefore not expressible in any word, not called by any name.

[62] Usener, *Götternamen*, p. 334.

[63] Cf. Brugsch, *Religion u. Mythologie der alten Aegypter*, Leipzig, 1888, p. 645; for the expression "Isis Myrionyma," which is found also in Latin inscriptions, see Wissowa, *Religion und Kultus der Römer*, Vol. 2, p. 91.—In magical practice, this concept of the "polynomy" of gods has become regular stock in trade; thus we find, in Graeco-Egyptian magic formulas and prayers, invocations of Dionysius and Apollo in which the several names whereby they are called are arranged in alphabetical order, so that each verse presents a letter of the alphabet. For details see Hopfner, *Griechisch-Aegyptischer Offenbarungszauber*, Sec. 684, p. 175.

[64] For details see Brinton, *Religions of Primitive Peoples*, p. 99.

Here the cycle of mythico-religious thinking is completed. But the beginning and the end do not resemble each other; for we have progressed from a realm of mere indeterminateness to the realm of true generality. The Divine, instead of entering into the welter of properties and proper names, the gay kaleidoscope of phenomena, is set off against this world as something without attributes. For every mere "attribute" would limit its pure essence; *omnis determinatio est negatio.* It is especially the cult of mysticism, in all ages and among all peoples, that grapples again and again with this intellectual double problem—the task of comprehending the Divine in its totality, in its highest inward reality, and yet avoiding any particularity of name or image. Thus all mysticism is directed toward a world beyond language, a world of silence. As Meister Eckhardt has written, God is "the simple ground, the still desert, the simple silence" (der einveltige grunt, die stille wueste, die einveltic stille"); for "that is his nature, that he is one nature."[65]

The spiritual depth and power of language is strikingly evinced in the fact that it is speech itself which prepares the way for that last step whereby it is itself transcended. This most difficult and peculiar achievement is represented by two fundamental, linguistically grounded concepts—the concept of "Being," and the concept of the "Ego." Both appear to belong, in their complete significance, to a relatively late development of language; both show, in their grammatical forms, clear traces of the difficulties which verbal expression encountered in face of these concepts, and could master only by slow degrees. In regard to the concept of Being, a glance at the development and the original etymological meaning

[65] See Fr. Pfeiffer, *Deutsche Mystiker des vierzehnten Jahrhunderts*, Vol. II: *Meister Eckhardt* (Leipzig, 1857), p. 160.

of the *copula* in most languages shows how verbally oriented thinking arrived only very gradually at a distinction between "being" and "being-so." The "is" of the copula almost unfailingly goes back to a sensuously concrete original meaning; instead of conveying mere existence or a general state of being, it originally denoted a particular kind and form of appearance; especially being in a certain place, at a specific point in space.[66]

Now, when the growth of language achieves the liberation of the concept of Being from its bondage to some specific *form* of existence, it thereby furnishes mythico-religious thought with a new vehicle, a new intellectual tool. Critical, or "discursive," thinking, it is true, finally progresses to a point at which the expression of "being" appears as the expression of a *relation*, so that, to speak with Kant, Being is no longer a "possible predicate of a thing," and therefore can no longer be an attribute of God. But for mythic thought, which recognizes no such critical distinction, but remains "substantive" even in its highest reaches, Being is not only a predicate, but at a certain stage of development actually becomes the Predicate of Predicates; it becomes the expression which allows one to subsume all the attributes of God under a single rubric. Wherever, in the history of religious thought, the demand for the *Unity* of the Deity arises, it takes its stand on the linguistic expression of Being, and finds its surest support in the Word. Even in Greek philosophy this course of religious thinking may still be traced; even in Xenophanes we find the Unity of God derived and proved from the Unity of Being. But this connection is by no means restricted to philosophical speculation; it goes back to the oldest known records in

[66] Illustrations of this principle may be found in my *Philosophie der symbolischen Formen*, Vol. I, pp. 287 ff.

the history of religion. In early Egyptian texts, in the midst of all the gods and animals of the Egyptian pantheon, we encounter the idea of the "hidden God," who is referred to in the inscriptions as the One whose form no one has known, whose image no one has discovered; "He is a secret to his creation," "His name is a secret to his children." There is but one designation that may be applied to him, besides that of Creator, Maker of men and gods: that is the designation of pure Being. He begets and is not begotten, he bears and is not born, he is Being, the Constant in everything, the Remaining in all. Thus he "Is from the beginning," "Is from the first"; everything that is, became after he was.[67] Here all separate, concrete and individual divine names have been resolved into the one name of Being; the Divine excludes from itself all particular attributes, it cannot be described through anything else, but can be predicated only of itself.

From here it is but a single step to the fundamental idea of true monotheism. This step is accomplished as soon as the unity which so far has been sought through the objective world, and expressed in objective terms, is turned into a subjective essence, and the meaning of divinity is approached not through the existence of things, but through the being of the Person, the Self. What has been said about the expression of "Being" may also be said about the denotation of the "I"—it had to be gradually found in the course of language making, and had to be derived, slowly and stepwise, from concrete, purely sensory beginnings. But as soon as the expression "I" is finally coined, religious thought has gained a new category. And again it is religious language

[67] Compare the excerpts and translations from inscriptions, in Brugsch, *Religion und Mythologie der alten Aegypter*, pp. 56ff., 96ff.

that seizes upon the new expression, and uses it, as it were, for a rung to reach a new spiritual height. The form of "self-predication," of self-revelation of the god through a constantly reiterated "I am . . . ," which reveals the various aspects of his unified being, originates in Egypt and Babylon; afterward, in later stages, it develops into a typical stylistic form of religious expression.[68] But its final form is not met with until it excludes all other forms; where, accordingly, the only "name" for the god is the name of the Self. When God, revealing himself to Moses, is asked what name Moses should bear to the Israelites, in case they want to know what god has sent him to them, the answer is: "I am that I am. Thus thou shalt say to them: I am has sent me unto you." It is only by this transformation of objective existence into subjective being that the Deity is really elevated to the "absolute" realm, to a state that cannot be expressed through any analogy with things or names of things. The only instruments of speech that remain for its expression are the personal pronouns: "I am he; I am the first, the last," as it is written in the Prophetic Books.[69]

Finally, both lines of contemplation—that which uses the notion of Being, and that which uses the notion of Self—are gathered up into one, in the speculations of India. This philosophy, too, takes its departure from the "Holy Word," the Brahma. In the Vedic books it is the power of this Holy Word to which all Being, even the gods, must submit. The Word rules and guides the course of nature; knowledge and possession of it gives the initiate

[68] For the origin and dissemination of this form see the exhaustive studies by Norden (instructive also for students of religious philosophy): *Agnostos Theos*, pp. 177 ff., 207 ff.

[69] Isaiah 48: 12; cf. 43: 10. For the significance of the "I am he," see Goldziher, *Der Mythos bei den Hebräern* (Leipzig, 1876), pp. 359 ff.

power over everything in the world. At first, it is treated entirely as a particular, to which some particular phase of existence is subject; in its use, the priest has to observe the most meticulous detail—any deviation by even a syllable, any change in rhythm or meter would void the potency of the prayer. But the progress from the Vedas to the Upanishads shows us how the Word is gradually liberated from this magic circle, and becomes an all-inclusive intellectual potency. From the essences of particular things, expressed in their separate concrete denotations, human thought rises to the unity that encompasses them all. The power of individual words is distilled, so to speak, into the power of the Word as such, the Brahma.[70] In this, all particular being, everything that seems to have a "nature" of its own, is represented; but by virtue of this inclusion it is at once divested of its "nature." In order to express this relationship, religious speculation is driven again to the concept of Being, which the Upanishads, seeking to grasp its abstract meaning, now present in a sort of heightened form, a higher potential. As Plato contrasted the ὄντα, the world of empirical things, with the ὄντως ὄν, the pure Being of the Idea, so we find in the Upanishads the world of particular existence opposed to the Brahma as the "Being-in-Being" ("satyasya satyam").[71]

This development presently meets and interpenetrates

[70] For the fundamental meaning of Brahma as the "Holy Word," as prayer and incantation, cf. Oldenberg, in the *Anzeiger für indogermanische Sprach= und Altertumskunde*, Vol. VIII, p. 40; also Oldenberg, *Die Religion der Upanishaden und die Anfänge des Buddhismus* (Göttingen 1915), pp. 17 ff., 38 ff., 46 ff. A somewhat divergent explanation is given by Hopkins, who regards the concept of power as the fundamental notion of Brahma, and believes this concept to have been transferred later to the word as prayer, with its magical potency. (Hopkins, *Origin and Evolution of Religion*, New Haven, 1923, p. 309.)

[71] Examples may be found in Deussen, *Philosophie der Upanishads* (Leipzig, 1899), pp. 119 ff.

with the other, which takes its departure from the opposite pole: the intellectual progression which treats not Being but Self as the keynote of religious thought. Both converge on the same goal; for Being and Self, Brahma and Atman, are distinct only in expression, not in content. The Self is the only thing that neither ages nor passes, that is unchangeable and immortal, and therefore is the true "Absolute." But by taking this final step, by identifying Brahma and Atman, religious thought and speculation has again broken its original bounds, the bounds of language. For words can no longer grasp and hold this unity of "subject" and "object." Language now vacillates *between* subjective and objective, it moves ever from one to the other, from the second back to the first; but this means that even in combining the two it always has to recognize them as separate ideas. When religious speculation denies this distinction, it claims independence from the power of the word and the guidance of language; but thereby it arrives at the transcendental, which is inaccessible not only to language, but to conception as well. The only name, the only denotation that remains for this Pan-Unity is the expression of negation. Being is Atman, who is called "No, no"; above this "It is not so" there is nothing further, nothing higher. So this revolt of the mind, which severs the bond between language and mythico-religious thought, only goes to demonstrate once more how strong and close is this bond; for as myth and religion seek to transcend the bourne of language, they arrive therewith at the limits of their own creative and formulative power.

When, in the year 1878, Max Müller published his *Lectures on the Origin and Growth of Religion*, he leaned heavily on the first reports he received by letter from Codrington concerning the mana of the Melanesians, which he used in support of his fundamental thesis in philosophy of religion—the thesis that all religion is grounded in the power of the human mind to grasp the "Infinite." "What I hold," he says, "is that with every finite perception there is a concomitant perception, or, if that word should seem too strong, a concomitant sentiment or presentiment of the infinite; that from the very first act of touch, or hearing, or sight, we are brought in contact, not only with a visible, but at the same time with an invisible universe."

And in the word "mana," which he interpreted as "a Polynesian name for the Infinite," he saw one of the earliest and clumsiest expressions of what Man's conception of the Infinite may have been in its most primitive stages.[72]

Our increasing acquaintance with the mythico-religious realm to which the conception and expression "mana" belongs has completely destroyed the nimbus of infinity and supersensoriness which surrounded the word, as Müller understood it; it has shown us how thoroughly the "religion" of mana is grounded not only in sense perception, but in sensual desires, in absolutely "finite" practical interests.[73] Indeed, Müller's interpretation is possible only because he equated the "infinite" with the "indefinite," the "interminable" with the "indeterminate."[74] But the fluidity of the mana concept, which makes it so hard for us to grasp, or to find any verbal

[72] See Friedrich Max Müller, *Lectures on the Origin and Growth of Religion* (New impression, London, 1898), pp. 46ff.

[73] "All Melanesian religion," says Müller, citing a letter of Codrington's, "in fact, consists in getting this Mana for oneself, or getting it used for one's benefit—all religion, that is, as far as religious practices go, prayers and sacrifices."

[74] "What I want to prove in this course of lectures is that indefinite and infinite are in reality two names for the same thing" (op. *cit.*, p. 36).

equivalent for it in our language pattern, has nothing whatever to do with the philosophical or religious idea of the Infinite. As the latter is *above* the possibility of exact verbal determination, so the former is still *below* such fixation. Language moves in the middle kingdom between the "indefinite" and the "infinite"; it transforms the indeterminate into a determinate idea, and then holds it within the sphere of finite determinations. So there are, in the realm of mythic and religious conception, "ineffables" of different order, one of which represents the lower limit of verbal expression, the other the upper limit; but between these bounds, which are drawn by the very nature of verbal expression, language can move with perfect freedom, and exhibit all the wealth and concrete exemplification of its creative power.

Here, again, the mythmaking mind exhibits a sort of consciousness of the relationship between its product and the phenomenon of language, though characteristically it can express this relationship not in abstract logical terms, but only in images. It transforms the spiritual dawn which takes place with the advent of language into an objective fact, and presents it as a cosmogonic process. Jean Paul remarks somewhere: " seems to me that, just as animals drift through the ou world as though it were a dark undulating sea, so n too, would be lost in the starry vastness of external ceptions, could he not divide that vague brightne constellations by the agency of language, and lve the whole into its parts for his consciousne ce from the vague fullness of exister r verbally determinable form hic mode, in the ima sition between at makes from the featureless matrix of Being to its form and organization. Thus the Babylonian-Assyrian myth of creation describes Chaos as the condition of the world when the heavens above were "unnamed" and on earth no name was known for any thing. In Egypt, too, the time before creation is called the time when no god existed and no name for any object was known.[75]

From this indefinite state arises the first determinate existence when the creator god utters his own name, and by virtue of the power dwelling in that word calls himself into being. The idea that this god is his own cause, a real *causa sui*, is mythically expressed in the story of his origin through the magical force of his name. Before him there was no god, nor was any god beside him, "there was for him no mother who made his name for him, nor father who uttered it, saying: 'I have begotten him.' "[76] In the Book of the Dead, the sun-god Râ is represented his own creator in that he gives himself his names, i.e., aracters and his powers.[77] And from this original speech which dwells in the demiurge arises se that has existence and definite being; he causes the birth of gods and men.[78] occurs, with a somewhat different turn eaning, in the Biblical account of

ulte divin journalier en Egypte (Paris,

Moret, *Mystères Egyptiens*, pp.

cf. Erman, *Die aegyptische*

given by M
stères

Creation. Here, too, it is the word of God that separates light from darkness and produces the heavens and the earth. But the names of earthly creatures are no longer directly given by the Creator, but have to wait their assignment by Man. After God has created all the beasts of the field and the fowls of the air he brings them to man, to see what he will call them. "And whatsoever Adam called every living creature, that was the name thereof." (Genesis 2: 19). In this act of appellation, man takes possession of the world both physically and intellectually—subjects it to his knowledge and his rule. This special feature reveals that fundamental character and spiritual achievement of pure monotheism of which Goethe remarked that it is always uplifting because the belief in the one and only God makes man aware of his own inner unity. This unity, however, cannot be discovered except as it reveals itself in outward form by virtue of the concrete structures of language and myth, in which it is embodied, and from which it is afterward regained by the process of logical reflection.

◦§ 6 §◦

The Power of Metaphor

THE foregoing considerations have shown us how mythical and verbal thought are interwoven in every way; how the great structures of the mythic and linguistic realms, respectively, are determined and guided through long periods of their development by the same spiritual motives. Yet one fundamental motive has so

far remained unnoticed, which not only illustrates their
relationship, but offers an ultimate explanation of it.
That myth and language are subject to the same, or at
least closely analogous, laws of evolution can really be
seen and understood only in so far as we can uncover
the common root from which both of them spring. The
resemblances in their results, in the forms which they
produce, point to a final community of function, of the
principles whereby they operate. In order to recognize
this function and represent it in its abstract nakedness,
we have to pursue the ways of myth and language not
in their progress, but in regress—back to the point from
which those two divergent lines emanate. And this common center really seems to be demonstrable; for, no matter how widely the contents of myth and language may
differ, yet the same form of mental conception is opera-
tive in both. It is the form which one may denote as
metaphorical thinking; the nature and meaning of
metaphor is what we must start with if we want to find,
on the one hand, the unity of the verbal and the mythical
worlds and, on the other, their difference.

It has frequently been noted that the intellectual link
between language and myth is metaphor; but in the
precise definition of the process, and even in regard to
the general direction it is supposed to take, theories are
widely at variance. The real source of metaphor is sought
now in the construction of language, now in mythic
imagination; sometimes it is supposed to be speech,
which by its originally metaphorical nature begets myth,
and is its eternal source; sometimes, on the contrary,
the metaphorical character of words is regarded as a
legacy which language has received from myth and holds
in fee. Herder, in his prize essay on the origin of speech,
emphasized the mythic aspect of all verbal and proposi-

tional conceptions. "As all nature sounds; so to Man, creature of sense, nothing could seem more natural than that it lives, and speaks, and acts. A certain savage sees a tree, with its majestic crown; the crown rustles! That is stirring godhead! The savage falls prostrate and worships! Behold the history of sensuous Man, that dark web, in its becoming, out of *verbis nomina*—and the easiest transition to abstract thought! For the savages of North America, for instance, everything is still animate; everything has its genius, its spirit. That it was likewise among Greeks and orientals, may be seen from their oldest dictionary and grammar—they are, as was all nature to their inventor, a pantheon! A realm of living, acting creatures. . . . The driving storm, the gentle zephyr, the clear fountain and the mighty ocean—their whole mythology lies in those treasure troves, in *verbis* and *nominibus* of the ancient languages; and the earliest dictionary was thus a sounding pantheon."[79]

The romantics followed the way indicated by Herder; Schelling, too, sees in language a "faded mythology," which preserves in formal and abstract distinctions what mythology still treats as living, concrete differences.[80] Exactly the opposite course was taken by the "comparative mythology" that was attempted in the second half of the nineteenth century, especially by Adalbert Kuhn and Max Müller. Since this school adopted the *methodological* principle of basing mythological comparisons on linguistic comparisons, the *factual* primacy of verbal concepts over mythic ones seemed to them to be implied in their procedure. Thus mythology appeared as a result of language. The "root metaphor" underlying all mythic

[79] "Ueber den Ursprung der Sprache," *Werke* (ed. Suphan), V, pp. 53 f.
[80] Schelling, "Einleitung in die Philosophie der Mythologie," *Sämtliche Werke*, 2nd div., I, p. 52.

formulations was regarded as an essentially verbal phenomenon, the basic character of which was to be investigated and understood. The homonymity or assonance of denotative terms was supposed to break and direct the way for mythic fantasy.

"Let us consider, then, that there was, necessarily and really, a period in the history of our race when all the thoughts that went beyond the narrow horizon of our everyday life had to be expressed by means of metaphors, and that these metaphors had not yet become what they are to us, mere conventional and traditional expressions, but were felt and understood half in their original and half in their modified character. . . . Whenever any word, that was at first used metaphorically, is used without a clear conception of the steps that led from its original to its metaphorical meaning, there is danger of mythology; whenever those steps are forgotten and artificial steps put in their places, we have mythology, or, if I may say so, we have diseased language, whether that language refers to religious or secular interests. . . . What is commonly called mythology is but a part of a much more general phase through which all language has at one time or other to pass."[81]

Before one can attempt any decision between these antagonistic theories, this battle for the priority of language over mythology or myth over language, the basic concept of metaphor requires scrutiny and definition. One can take it in a narrow sense, in which it comprises only the *conscious* denotation of one thought content by the name of another which resembles the former in some respect, or is somehow analogous to it. In that case, metaphor is a genuine "translation"; the two concepts

---

[81] Max Müller, *Lectures on the Science of Language*, second series (New York: Scribner, Armstrong & Co., 1875), pp. 372-376.

between which it obtains are fixed and independent meanings, and betwixt them, as the given *terminus a quo* and *terminus ad quem*, the conceptual process takes place, which causes the transition from one to the other, whereby one is semantically made to stand proxy for the other. Any attempt to probe the generic causes of this conceptual and nominal substitution, and to explain the extraordinarily wide and variegated use of this sort of metaphor (i.e., the conscious identification of avowedly diverse objects), especially in primitive forms of thinking and speaking, leads one back to an essential attitude of mythic thought and feeling. Heinz Werner, in his study of the origins of metaphor, has presented a very plausible argument for the supposition that this particular kind of metaphor, the circumlocution of one idea in terms of another, rests on quite definite motives arising from the magical view of the world, and more especially from certain name and word taboos.[82]

But such a use of metaphor clearly presupposes that both the ideas and their verbal correlates are already given as definite quantities; only if these elements, as such, are verbally fixed and defined can they be exchanged for one another. Such transposition and substitution, which operate with a previously known vocabulary as their material, must be clearly distinguished from that genuine "radical metaphor" which is a condition of the very formulation of mythic as well as verbal conceptions. Indeed, even the most primitive verbal utterance requires a transmutation of a certain cognitive or emotive experience into sound, i.e., into a medium that is foreign to the experience, and even quite disparate; just as the simplest mythical form can arise only

[82] Heinz Werner, *Die Ursprünge der Metapher* (Leipzig, 1919), esp. chap. 3, pp. 74 ff.

by virtue of a transformation which removes a certain impression from the realm of the ordinary, the everyday and profane, and lifts it to the level of the "holy," the sphere of mythico-religious "significance." This involves not merely a transference, but a real μετάβασις εἰς ἄλλο γένος; in fact, it is not only a transition to another category, but actually the creation of the category itself.

If, now, one were to ask which of these two types of metaphor begets the other—whether the metaphorical expressions in speech are produced by the mythic point of view, or whether, on the contrary, this point of view could arise and develop only on the basis of language— the foregoing considerations show that this question is really specious. For, in the first place, we are not dealing here with a temporal relation of "before" and "after," but with the logical relation between the forms of language and of myth, respectively; with the way the one conditions and determines the other. This determination, however, can be conceived only as reciprocal. Language and myth stand in an original and indissoluble correlation with one another, from which they both emerge but gradually as independent elements. They are two diverse shoots from the same parent stem, the same impulse of symbolic formulation, springing from the same basic mental activity, a concentration and heightening of simple sensory experience. In the vocables of speech and in primitive mythic figurations, the same inner process finds its consummation: they are both resolutions of an inner tension, the representation of subjective impulses and excitations in definite objective forms and figures. As Usener emphatically said: "It is not by any volition that the name of a thing is determined. People do not invent some arbitrary sound-complex, in order to introduce it as the sign of a certain object, as one might do with a token. The spiritual excitement caused by some object which presents itself in the outer world furnishes both the occasion and the means of its denomination. Sense impressions are what the self receives from its encounter with the not-self, and the liveliest of these naturally strive for vocal expression; they are the bases of the separate appellations which the speaking populace attempts."[83]

Now this genesis corresponds precisely, feature for feature, with that of the "momentary gods." Similarly, the significance of linguistic and mythic metaphors, respectively, will reveal itself, so that the spiritual power embodied in them may be properly understood, only as we trace them back to their common origin; if one seeks this significance and power in that peculiar concentration, that "intensification" of sense experience which underlies all linguistic as well as all mythico-religious formulations.

If we take our departure once more from the contrast which theoretical or "discursive" conception presents, we shall find indeed that the different *directions* which the growth of logical (discursive) and mythic-linguistic conception, respectively, have followed, may be seen just as clearly in their several *results*. The former begins with some individual, single perception, which we expand, and carry beyond its original bounds, by viewing it in more and more relationships. The intellectual process here involved is one of *synthetic supplementation*, the combination of the single instance with the totality, and its completion in the totality. But by this relationship with the whole, the separate fact does not lose its concrete identity and limitation. It fits into the sum total of phenomena, yet remains set off from them as something

[83] Usener, *Götternamen*, p. 3.

independent and singular. The ever-growing relationship which connects an individual perception with others does not cause it to become merged with the others. Each separate "specimen" of a species is "contained" in the species; the species itself is "subsumed" under a higher genus; but this means, also, that they remain distinct, they do not coincide. This fundamental relation is most readily and clearly expressed in the scheme which logicians are wont to use for the representation of the hierarchy of concepts, the order of inclusion and subsumption obtaining among genera and species. Here the logical determinations are represented as geometric determinations; every concept has a certain "area" that belongs to it and whereby it is distinguished from other conceptual spheres. No matter how much these areas may overlap, cover each other or interpenetrate—each one maintains its definitely bounded location in conceptual space. A concept maintains its sphere despite all its synthetic supplementation and extension; the new relations into which it may enter do not cause its boundaries to become effaced, but lead rather to their more distinct recognition.

If, now, we contrast this form of logical conception by species and genera with the primitive form of mythic and linguistic conception, we find immediately that the two represent entirely different *tendencies* of thought. Whereas in the former a concentric expansion over everwidening spheres of perception and conception takes place, we find exactly the opposite movement of thought giving rise to mythic ideation. The mental view is not widened, but compressed; it is, so to speak, distilled into a single point. Only by this process of distillation is the particular essence found and extracted which is to bear the special accent of "significance." All light is concentrated in one focal point of "meaning," while everything that lies outside these focal points of verbal or mythic conception remains practically invisible. It remains "un-remarked" because, and in so far as, it remains unsup-plied with any linguistic or mythic "marker." In the realm of discursive conception there reigns a sort of diffuse light—and the further logical analysis proceeds, the further does this even clarity and luminosity extend. But in the ideational realm of myth and language there are always, besides those locations from which the strongest light proceeds, others that appear wrapped in profoundest darkness. While certain contents of percep-tion become verbal-mythical centers of force, centers of significance, there are others which remain, one might say, beneath the threshold of meaning. This fact, namely, that primitive mythical and linguistic concepts constitute such *punctiform* units, accounts for the fact that they do not permit of any further *quantitative* distinctions. Logical contemplation always has to be carefully directed toward the *extension* of concepts; classical syllogistic logic is ultimately nothing but a system of rules for combining, subsuming and superimposing concepts. But the conceptions embodied in language and myth must be taken not in extension, but in intension; not quanti-tatively, but qualitatively. Quantity is reduced to a purely casual property, a relatively immaterial and unim-portant aspect. Two logical concepts, subsumed under the next-higher category, as their *genus proximum*, retain their distinctive characters despite the relationship into which they have been brought. In mythico-linguistic thought, however, exactly the opposite tendency pre-vails. Here we find in operation a law which might actually be called the law of the leveling and extinction of specific differences. Every part of a whole is the whole

itself; every specimen is equivalent to the entire species.
The part does not merely represent the whole, or the
specimen its class; they are identical with the totality to
which they belong; not merely as mediating aids to
reflective thought, but as genuine presences which actually contain the power, significance and efficacy of the
whole. Here one is reminded forcefully of the principle
which might be called the basic principle of verbal as well
as mythic "metaphor"—the principle of *pars pro toto*.
It is a familiar fact that all mythic thinking is governed
and permeated by this principle. Whoever has brought
any part of a whole into his power has thereby acquired
power, in the magical sense, over the whole itself. What
significance the part in question may have in the structure and coherence of the whole, what function it fulfills,
is relatively unimportant—the mere fact that it is or has
been a part, that it has been connected with the whole,
no matter how casually, is enough to lend it the full
significance and power of that greater unity. For instance,
to hold magical dominion over another person's body
one need only attain possession of his pared nails or
cut-off hair, his spittle or his excrement; even his shadow,
his reflection or his footprints serve the same purpose.
The Pythagoreans still observed the injunction to smooth
the bed soon after arising so that the imprint of the
body, left upon the mattress, could not be used to the
owner's detriment.[84] Most of what is known as "magic
of analogy" springs from the same fundamental attitude;
and the very nature of this magic shows that the concept
in question is not one of mere analogy, but of a real
identification. If, for instance, a rain-making ceremony
consists of sprinkling water on the ground to attract the

[84] Jamblichos, *Protreptichos* p. 108, 3, quoted after Deubner, *Magie und Religion* (Freiburg, 1922), p. 8.

rain, or rain-stopping magic is made by pouring water on red hot stones where it is consumed amid hissing noise,[85] both ceremonies owe their true magical sense to the fact that the rain is not just represented, but is felt to be really present in each drop of water. The rain as a mythic "power," the "daemon" of the rain is actually there, whole and undivided, in the sprinkled or evaporated water, and is thus amenable to magical control.

This mystic relationship which obtains between a whole and its parts holds also between genus and species, and between the species and its several instances. Here, too, each form is entirely merged with the other; the genus or species is not only represented by an individual member of it, but lives and acts in it. If, under the totemistic conception of the world, a group or clan is organized by totems, and if its individual members take their names from the totem animal or plant, this is never a mere arbitrary division by means of conventional verbal or mythical "insignia," but a matter of genuine community of essence.[86] In other respects, too, wherever a genus is involved at all, it always appears to be wholly present and wholly effective. The god or daemon of vegetation lives in each individual sheaf of the harvest. Therefore, an ancient but still popular rural custom demands that the last sheaf be left out in the field; in this remnant, the power of the fertility-god is concentrated, from which the harvest of the coming year is to grow.[87] In Mexico and among the Cora Indians the corn-god is supposed to be present, fully and unrestrictedly, in every

[85] See Parkinson, *Thirty Years in the South Seas*, p. 7; quoted by Werner, *Die Ursprünge der Metapher*, p. 56.

[86] Cf. my study, *Die Begriffsform im mythischen Denken* (Leipzig, 1922), pp. 16ff.

[87] Cf. Mannhardt, *Wald= und Feldkulte*, 2nd ed. (Berlin, 1904-1905), I, 212ff.

stalk and even every grain of corn. The Mexican corn-goddess Chicomecoatl in her maidenhood is the green stalk, in her old age the corn harvest; but she is also each separate kernel and each particular dish. Likewise, there are several deities among the Coras who represent certain kinds of flowers, but are addressed as individual flowers. The same is true of all the Coras' demoniac creatures: the cicada, the cricket, the grasshopper, the armadillo are simply treated as so many individual wholes.[88] If, therefore, ancient rhetoric names as one of the principal types of metaphor the substitution of a part for the whole, or vice versa, it is easy enough to see how *this* sort of metaphor arises directly out of the essential attitude of the mythic mind. But it is equally clear that for mythic thinking there is much more in metaphor than a bare "substitution," a mere rhetorical figure of speech; that what seems to our subsequent reflection as a sheer transcription is mythically conceived as a genuine and direct identification.[89]

[88] See Preuss, in *Globus*, Vol. 87, p. 381; cf. esp. *Die Nayarit-Expedition*, Vol. I, pp. 47 ff.

[89] This is the more obviously valid if we consider that for mythic and magical thought there is no such thing as a mere picture, since every image embodies the "nature" of its object, i.e., its "soul" or "daemon." Cf., for example, Budge, *Egyptian Magic*, p. 65: "It has been said above that the name or the emblem or the picture of a god or a demon could become an amulet with power to protect him that wore it and that such power lasted as long as the substance of which it was made lasted, if the name, or emblem, or picture was not erased from it. But the Egyptians went a step further than this and they believed that it was possible to transmit to the figure of any man, or woman, or animal or living creature the soul of the being which it represented, and its qualities and attributes. The statue of a god in a temple contained the spirit of the god which it represented, and from time immemorial the people of Egypt believed that every statue and figure possessed an indwelling spirit." The same belief is held to this day among all "primitive" peoples. Cf., for instance, Hetherwick, "Some animistic beliefs among the Yaos of British Central Africa" (see footnote above, p. 70): "The photographic camera was at first an object of dread, and when it was turned upon a group of natives

In the light of this basic principle of mythic metaphor we can grasp and understand, somewhat more clearly, what is commonly called the metaphorical function of language. Even Quintilian pointed out that this function does not constitute any *part* of speech, but that it governs and characterizes all human talk; *paene quidquid loquimur figura est*. But if this is indeed the case—if metaphor, taken in this general sense, is not just a certain development of speech, but must be regarded as one of its essential conditions—then any effort to understand its function leads us back, once more, to the fundamental form of verbal *conceiving*. Such conceiving stems ultimately from that same process of concentration, the compression of given sense experiences, which originally initiates every single verbal concept. If we assume that this sort of concentration occurs by virtue of several experiences, and along several lines, so that two different perceptual complexes might yield the same sort of "essence" as their inner significance, which *gives* them their meaning, then at this very point we should expect that first and firmest of all the connections which language can establish; for, as the nameless simply has no existence in language, but tends to be completely obscured, so whatever things bear the *same* appellation appear absolutely similar. The similarity of the aspect fixed by the word causes all other heterogeneity among the perceptions in question to become more and more obscured, and finally to vanish altogether. Here again, a part usurps the place of the whole—indeed, it becomes and is the whole. By virtue of the "equivalence" principle, entities

---

they scattered in all directions with shrieks of terror . . . In their minds the *lisoka* (soul) was allied to the *chiwilili* or picture and the removal of it to the photographic plate would mean the disease or death of the shadeless body" (pp. 89 f.).

which appear entirely diverse in direct sense perception
or from the standpoint of logical classification may be
treated as similars in language, so that every statement
made about one of them may be transferred and applied
to the other. Preuss, in a characterization of magic-
complex thinking, says: "If the Cora Indian classes butterflies, quite absurdly, as birds, this means that all the
properties which he notes in the object are quite differ-
ently classified and related for him than they are for us
from our analytical, scientific point of view."[90] But the
apparent absurdity of this and other such classifications
disappears as soon as we realize that the formation of
these primary concepts was guided by language. If we
suppose that the element emphasized in the name, and
therefore in the verbal concept of "bird," as an essential
characteristic was the element of "flight," then by virtue
of this element and by its mediation the butterfly does
belong to the class of birds. Our own languages are still
constantly producing such classifications, which contra-
dict our empirical and scientific concepts of species and
genera, as for instance the denotation "butterfly" (Dutch
botervlieg), in some Germanic tongues called a "butter-
bird." And at the same time one can see how such
lingual "metaphors" react in their turn on mythic metaphor and prove to be an ever-fertile source for the latter.
Every characteristic property which once gave a point
of departure to qualifying conceptions and qualifying
appellations may now serve to merge and identify the
objects denoted by these names. If the visible image of
lightning, as it is fixed by language, is concentrated upon
the impression of "serpentine," this causes the lightning
to *become a snake*; if the sun is called "the heavenly
flier," it appears henceforth as an arrow or a bird—the

[90] Preuss, *Die geistige Kultur der Naturvölker* (Leipzig, 1914), p. 10.

sun-god of the Egyptian pantheon, for instance, who is represented with a falcon's head. For in this realm of thought there are no abstract denotations; every word is immediately transformed into a concrete mythical figure, a god or a daemon. Any sense impression, no matter how vague, if it be fixed and held in language, may thus become a starting point for the conception and denotation of a god. Among the names of the Lithuanian gods which Usener has listed, the snow-god Blizgulis, the "Shimmerer," appears beside the god of cattle, the "Roarer" Baubis; also in relation to these we find the god of bees, Birbullis the "Hummer," and the god of earthquake, the "Thresher" Drebkulys.[91] Once a "Roarer God" in this sense was conceived, he could not but be recognized in the most diverse guises; he was naturally and directly *heard*, in the voice of the lion as in the roaring of the storm and the thunder of the ocean. Again and again, in this respect, myth receives new life and wealth from language, as language does from myth. And this constant interaction and interpenetration attests the unity of the mental principle from which both are sprung, and of which they are simply different expressions, different manifestations and grades.

Yet in the advance of human mentality even this conjunction, close and essential though it seems to be, begins to disintegrate and dissolve. For language does not belong exclusively to the realm of myth; it bears within itself, from its very beginning, another power, the power of logic. How this power gradually waxes great, and breaks its way by means of language, we cannot undertake to set forth here. But in the course of that evolution, words are reduced more and more to the status of mere conceptual signs. And this process of

[91] Usener, *Götternamen*, pp. 85 ff., 114.

separation and liberation is paralleled by another: art, like language, is originally bound up entirely with myth. Myth, language and art begin as a concrete, undivided unity, which is only gradually resolved into a triad of independent modes of spiritual creativity. Consequently, the same mythic animation and hypostatization which is bestowed upon the words of human speech is originally accorded to *images*, to every kind of artistic representation. Especially in the magical realm, word magic is everywhere accompanied by picture magic.[92] The image, too, achieves its purely representative, specifically "aesthetic" function only as the magic circle with which mythical consciousness surrounds it is broken, and it is recognized not as a mythico-magical form, but as a particular sort of *formulation*.

But although language and art both become emancipated, in this fashion, from their native soil of mythical thinking, the ideal, spiritual unity of the two is reasserted upon a higher level. If language is to grow into a vehicle of thought, an expression of concepts and judgments, this evolution can be achieved only at the price of forgoing the wealth and fullness of immediate experience. In the end, what is left of the concrete sense and feeling content it once possessed is little more than a bare skeleton. But there is one intellectual realm in which the word not only preserves its original creative power, but is ever renewing it; in which it undergoes a sort of constant palingenesis, at once a sensuous and a spiritual reincarnation. This regeneration is achieved as language becomes an avenue of artistic expression. Here it recovers the fullness of life; but it is no longer a life mythically bound and fettered, but an aesthetically liberated life.

[92] For further details see the second volume of my *Philosophie der symbolischen Formen*, esp. pp. 54ff.

Among all types and forms of poetry, the lyric is the one which most clearly mirrors this ideal development. For lyric poetry is not only rooted in mythic motives as its beginning, but keeps its connection with myth even in its highest and purest products. The greatest lyric poets, for instance Hölderlin or Keats, are men in whom the mythic power of insight breaks forth again in its full intensity and objectifying power. But this objectivity has discarded all material constraints. The spirit lives in the word of language and in the mythical image without falling under the control of either. What poetry expresses is neither the mythic word-picture of gods and daemons, nor the logical truth of abstract determinations and relations. The world of poetry stands apart from both, as a world of illusion and fantasy—but it is just in this mode of illusion that the realm of pure feeling can find utterance, and can therewith attain its full and concrete actualization. Word and mythic image, which once confronted the human mind as hard realistic powers, have now cast off all reality and effectuality; they have become a light, bright ether in which the spirit can move without let or hindrance. This liberation is achieved not because the mind throws aside the sensuous forms of word and image, but in that it uses them both as organs of its own, and thereby recognizes them for what they really are: forms of its own self-revelation.

INDEX

Achelis, 47n
Aeschylos, 59
Animal mind, 38, 81
Art, 98
Australians, 52n

Bantu, 39, 53n, 69, 71, 72n
Bastian, quoted, 47-48n
Beth, 59n
Brahma, 77
Breysig, K., 60n
Brinton, B., 6n, 48n, 50n, 71n,
    73n
Brugsch, 73n
Budge, 49n, 50n
    quoted, 94n
Bundahish, 47

Chinese, 50
Codrington, 62f, 65, 79
Concepts, 7, 12
    historical 27f
    linguistic, 24, 30, 32, 39f, 44,
        55
    mythical, 10, 14, 23, 32f
    religious, 14, 15, chapter 2
        passim
    scientific, 27f
Cuoq, 51n

Dempwolff, O., 41n
Descartes, R., 11
Deubner, 92n
Deussen, 78n
Dieterich, quoted, 53f

Eckhardt, quoted, 74
Egyptian
    magic, 94n
    religion, 46, 48f, 76, 97
Erman, 82n
    quoted, 48n
    use of names, 50, 73, 77, 82

Eskimos, 50
Evé, 22f, 34, 42, 52, 59
Foucart, G., quoted, 49n

Gabelentz, G. v. d., 50
Gelder, 48n
Giesebrecht, 51n, 53
God, 46, 70, 74ff, 83
Gods, 13, 14, 46, 59, 71n, 73, 94
    functional, 19f, 36, 41
    momentary, 18, 33, 35f, 42, 57,
        62, 71, 89
    special, 19ff, 42, 54
Goethe, J. W., 27, 83
Goldziher, 77n
Greek
    language, 4, 5, 31
    religion, 18, 20ff, 59
    word-magic, 52, 53n, 54, 82

Hamann, 34
Hartland, 72n
Herder, J. G., 84
    quoted, 29f, 85
Herero, 39
Hermippos, quoted, 52n
Hetherwick, quoted, 70n, 71n,
    94n
Hewitt, 64n, 65n, 72n
Hirzel, R., 51n
Hölderlin, 99
Hopfner, 49n, 73n
    quoted, 53n
Hopkins, 78n
Howitt, 52n
Humboldt, W. v., 30
    quoted, 9

India, philosophy of, 47, 77
Indians
    Algonquin, 51, 64, 67ff, 71
    Cherokee, 61

101

A CATALOG OF SELECTED
DOVER BOOKS
IN ALL FIELDS OF INTEREST

A CATALOG OF SELECTED DOVER
BOOKS IN ALL FIELDS OF INTEREST

LASERS AND HOLOGRAPHY, Winston E. Kock. Sound introduction to burgeoning field, expanded (1981) for second edition. 84 illustrations. 160pp. 5⅜ × 8¼. (EUK)   24041-X Pa. $3.50

FLORAL STAINED GLASS PATTERN BOOK, Ed Sibbett, Jr. 96 exquisite floral patterns—irises, poppie, lilies, tulips, geometrics, abstracts, etc.—adaptable to innumerable stained glass projects. 64pp. 8¼ × 11.   24259-5 Pa. $3.50

THE HISTORY OF THE LEWIS AND CLARK EXPEDITION, Meriwether Lewis and William Clark. Edited by Eliott Coues. Great classic edition of Lewis and Clark's day-by-day journals. Complete 1893 edition, edited by Eliott Coues from Biddle's authorized 1814 history. 1508pp. 5⅜ × 8½.
21268-8, 21269-6, 21270-X Pa. Three-vol. set $22.50

ORLEY FARM, Anthony Trollope. Three-dimensional tale of great criminal case. Original Millais illustrations illuminate marvelous panorama of Victorian society. Plot was author's favorite. 736pp. 5⅜ × 8½.   24181-5 Pa. $10.95

THE CLAVERINGS, Anthony Trollope. Major novel, chronicling aspects of British Victorian society, personalities. 16 plates by M. Edwards; first reprint of full text. 412pp. 5⅜ × 8½.   23464-9 Pa. $6.00

EINSTEIN'S THEORY OF RELATIVITY, Max Born. Finest semi-technical account; much explanation of ideas and math not readily available elsewhere on this level. 376pp. 5⅜ × 8½.   60769-0 Pa. $5.00

COMPUTABILITY AND UNSOLVABILITY, Martin Davis. Classic graduate-level introduction th theory of computability, usually referred to as theory of recurrent functions. New preface and appendix. 288pp. 5⅜ × 8½. 61471-9 Pa. $6.50

THE GODS OF THE EGYPTIANS, E.A. Wallis Budge. Never excelled for richness, fullness: all gods, goddesses, demons, mythical figures of Ancient Egypt; their legends, rites, incarnations, etc. Over 225 illustrations, plus 6 color plates. 988pp. 6⅛ × 9¼. (EBE)   22055-9, 22056-7 Pa., Two-vol. set $20.00

THE I CHING (THE BOOK OF CHANGES), translated by James Legge. Most penetrating divination manual ever prepared. Indispensable to study of early Oriental civilizations, to modern inquiring reader. 448pp. 5⅜ × 8½.
21062-6 Pa. $6.50

THE CRAFTSMAN'S HANDBOOK, Cennino Cennini. 15th-century handbook, school of Giotto, explains applying gold, silver leaf; gesso; fresco painting, grinding pigments, etc. 142pp. 6⅛ × 9¼.   20054-X Pa. $3.50

AN ATLAS OF ANATOMY FOR ARTISTS, Fritz Schider. Finest text, working book. Full text, plus anatomical illustrations; plates by great artists showing anatomy. 593 illustrations. 192pp. 7⅛ × 10¼.   20241-0 Pa. $6.50

EASY-TO-MAKE STAINED GLASS LIGHTCATCHERS, Ed Sibbett, Jr. 67 designs for most enjoyable ornaments: fruits, birds, teddy bears, trumpet, etc. Full size templates. 64pp. 8¼ × 11.   24081-9 Pa. $3.95

TRIAD OPTICAL ILLUSIONS AND HOW TO DESIGN THEM, Harry Turner. Triad explained in 32 pages of text, with 32 pages of Escher-like patterns on coloring stock. 92 figures. 32 plates. 64pp. 8¼ × 11.   23549-1 Pa. $2.95

SMOCKING: TECHNIQUE, PROJECTS, AND DESIGNS, Dianne Durand. Foremost smocking designer provides complete instructions on how to smock. Over 10 projects, over 100 illustrations. 56pp. 8¼ × 11. 23788-5 Pa. $2.00

AUDUBON'S BIRDS IN COLOR FOR DECOUPAGE, edited by Eleanor H. Rawlings. 24 sheets, 37 most decorative birds, full color, on one side of paper. Instructions, including work under glass. 56pp. 8¼ × 11. 23492-4 Pa. $3.95

THE COMPLETE BOOK OF SILK SCREEN PRINTING PRODUCTION, J.I. Biegeleisen. For commercial user, teacher in advanced classes, serious hobbyist. Most modern techniques, materials, equipment for optimal results. 124 illustrations. 253pp. 5⅜ × 8½. 21100-2 Pa. $4.50

A TREASURY OF ART NOUVEAU DESIGN AND ORNAMENT, edited by Carol Belanger Grafton. 577 designs for the practicing artist. Full-page, spots, borders, bookplates by Klimt, Bradley, others. 144pp. 8⅜ × 11¼. 24001-0 Pa. $5.95

ART NOUVEAU TYPOGRAPHIC ORNAMENTS, Dan X. Solo. Over 800 Art Nouveau florals, swirls, women, animals, borders, scrolls, wreaths, spots and dingbats, copyright-free. 100pp. 8⅛ × 11. 24366-4 Pa. $4.00

HAND SHADOWS TO BE THROWN UPON THE WALL, Henry Bursill. Wonderful Victorian novelty tells how to make flying birds, dog, goose, deer, and 14 others, each explained by a full-page illustration. 32pp. 6½ × 9¼. 21779-5 Pa. $1.50

AUDUBON'S BIRDS OF AMERICA COLORING BOOK, John James Audubon. Rendered for coloring by Paul Kennedy. 46 of Audubon's noted illustrations: red-wingèd black-bird, cardinal, etc. Original plates reproduced in full-color on the covers. Captions. 48pp. 8¼ × 11. 23049-X Pa. $2.25

SILK SCREEN TECHNIQUES, J.I. Biegeleisen, M.A. Cohn. Clear, practical, modern, economical. Minimal equipment (self-built), materials, easy methods. For amateur, hobbyist, 1st book. 141 illustrations. 185pp. 6⅛ × 9¼. 20433-2 Pa. $3.95

101 PATCHWORK PATTERNS, Ruby S. McKim. 101 beautiful, immediately useable patterns, full-size, modern and traditional. Also general information, estimating, quilt lore. 140 illustrations. 124pp. 7⅞ × 10¾. 20773-0 Pa. $3.50

READY-TO-USE FLORAL DESIGNS, Ed Sibbett, Jr. Over 100 floral designs (most in three sizes) of popular individual blossoms as well as bouquets, sprays, garlands. 64pp. 8¼ × 11. 23976-4 Pa. $2.95

AMERICAN WILD FLOWERS COLORING BOOK, Paul Kennedy. Planned coverage of 46 most important wildflowers, from Rickett's collection; instructive as well as entertaining. Color versions on covers. Captions. 48pp. 8¼ × 11. 20095-7 Pa. $2.50

CARVING DUCK DECOYS, Harry V. Shourds and Anthony Hillman. Detailed instructions and full-size templates for constructing 16 beautiful, marvelously practical decoys according to time-honored South Jersey method. 70pp. 9¼ × 12¼. 24083-5 Pa. $4.95

TRADITIONAL PATCHWORK PATTERNS, Carol Belanger Grafton. Cardboard cut-out pieces for use as templates to make 12 quilts: Buttercup, Ribbon Border, Tree of Paradise, nine more. Full instructions. 57pp. 8¼ × 11. 23015-5 Pa. $3.50

25 KITES THAT FLY, Leslie Hunt. Full, easy-to-follow instructions for kites made from inexpensive materials. Many novelties. 70 illustrations. 110pp. 5⅜ × 8½.
22550-X Pa. $2.25

PIANO TUNING, J. Cree Fischer. Clearest, best book for beginner, amateur. Simple repairs, raising dropped notes, tuning by easy method of flattened fifths. No previous skills needed. 4 illustrations. 201pp. 5⅜ × 8½.
23267-0 Pa. $3.50

EARLY AMERICAN IRON-ON TRANSFER PATTERNS, edited by Rita Weiss. 75 designs, borders, alphabets, from traditional American sources. 48pp. 8¼ × 11.
23162-3 Pa. $1.95

CROCHETING EDGINGS, edited by Rita Weiss. Over 100 of the best designs for these lovely trims for a host of household items. Complete instructions, illustrations. 48pp. 8¼ × 11.
24031-2 Pa. $2.25

FINGER PLAYS FOR NURSERY AND KINDERGARTEN, Emilie Poulsson. 18 finger plays with music (voice and piano); entertaining, instructive. Counting, nature lore, etc. Victorian classic. 53 illustrations. 80pp. 6½ × 9¼. 22588-7 Pa. $1.95

BOSTON THEN AND NOW, Peter Vanderwarker. Here in 59 side-by-side views are photographic documentations of the city's past and present. 119 photographs. Full captions. 122pp. 8¼ × 11.
24312-5 Pa. $6.95

CROCHETING BEDSPREADS, edited by Rita Weiss. 22 patterns, originally published in three instruction books 1939-41. 39 photos, 8 charts. Instructions. 48pp. 8¼ × 11.
23610-2 Pa. $2.00

HAWTHORNE ON PAINTING, Charles W. Hawthorne. Collected from notes taken by students at famous Cape Cod School; hundreds of direct, personal *apercus*, ideas, suggestions. 91pp. 5⅜ × 8½.
20653-X Pa. $2.50

THERMODYNAMICS, Enrico Fermi. A classic of modern science. Clear, organized treatment of systems, first and second laws, entropy, thermodynamic potentials, etc. Calculus required. 160pp. 5⅜ × 8½.
60361-X Pa. $4.00

TEN BOOKS ON ARCHITECTURE, Vitruvius. The most important book ever written on architecture. Early Roman aesthetics, technology, classical orders, site selection, all other aspects. Morgan translation. 331pp. 5⅜ × 8½. 20645-9 Pa. $5.50

THE CORNELL BREAD BOOK, Clive M. McCay and Jeanette B. McCay. Famed high-protein recipe incorporated into breads, rolls, buns, coffee cakes, pizza, pie crusts, more. Nearly 50 illustrations. 48pp. 8¼ × 11.
23995-0 Pa. $2.00

THE CRAFTSMAN'S HANDBOOK, Cennino Cennini. 15th-century handbook, school of Giotto, explains applying gold, silver leaf; gesso; fresco painting, grinding pigments, etc. 142pp. 6⅛ × 9¼.
20054-X Pa. $3.50

FRANK LLOYD WRIGHT'S FALLINGWATER, Donald Hoffmann. Full story of Wright's masterwork at Bear Run, Pa. 100 photographs of site, construction, and details of completed structure. 112pp. 9¼ × 10.
23671-4 Pa. $6.95

OVAL STAINED GLASS PATTERN BOOK, C. Eaton. 60 new designs framed in shape of an oval. Greater complexity, challenge with sinuous cats, birds, mandalas framed in antique shape. 64pp. 8¼ × 11.
24519-5 Pa. $3.50

CHILDREN'S BOOKPLATES AND LABELS, Ed Sibbett, Jr. 6 each of 12 types based on *Wizard of Oz, Alice,* nursery rhymes, fairy tales. Perforated; full color. 24pp. 8¼ × 11. 23538-6 Pa. $3.50

READY-TO-USE VICTORIAN COLOR STICKERS: 96 Pressure-Sensitive Seals, Carol Belanger Grafton. Drawn from authentic period sources. Motifs include heads of men, women, children, plus florals, animals, birds, more. Will adhere to any clean surface. 8pp. 8½ × 11. 24551-9 Pa. $2.95

CUT AND FOLD PAPER SPACESHIPS THAT FLY, Michael Grater. 16 colorful, easy-to-build spaceships that really fly. Star Shuttle, Lunar Freighter, Star Probe, 13 others. 32pp. 8¼ × 11. 23978-0 Pa. $2.50

CUT AND ASSEMBLE PAPER AIRPLANES THAT FLY, Arthur Baker. 8 aerodynamically sound, ready-to-build paper airplanes, designed with latest techniques. Fly *Pegasus, Daedalus, Songbird,* 5 other aircraft. Instructions. 32pp. 9¼ × 11¼. 24302-8 Pa. $3.95

SIDELIGHTS ON RELATIVITY, Albert Einstein. Two lectures delivered in 1920-21: *Ether and Relativity* and *Geometry and Experience.* Elegant ideas in non-mathematical form. 56pp. 5⅜ × 8½. 24511-X Pa. $2.25

FADS AND FALLACIES IN THE NAME OF SCIENCE, Martin Gardner. Fair, witty appraisal of cranks and quacks of science: Velikovsky, orgone energy, Bridey Murphy, medical fads, etc. 373pp. 5⅜ × 8½. 20394-8 Pa. $5.95

VACATION HOMES AND CABINS, U.S. Dept. of Agriculture. Complete plans for 16 cabins, vacation homes and other shelters. 105pp. 9 × 12. 23631-5 Pa. $4.95

HOW TO BUILD A WOOD-FRAME HOUSE, L.O. Anderson. Placement, foundations, framing, sheathing, roof, insulation, plaster, finishing—almost everything else. 179 illustrations. 223pp. 7⅞ × 10¾. 22954-8 Pa. $5.50

THE MYSTERY OF A HANSOM CAB, Fergus W. Hume. Bizarre murder in a hansom cab leads to engrossing investigation. Memorable characters, rich atmosphere. 19th-century bestseller, still enjoyable, exciting. 256pp. 5⅜ × 8. 21956-9 Pa. $4.00

MANUAL OF TRADITIONAL WOOD CARVING, edited by Paul N. Hasluck. Possibly the best book in English on the craft of wood carving. Practical instructions, along with 1,146 working drawings and photographic illustrations. 576pp. 6½ × 9¼. 23489-4 Pa. $8.95

WHITTLING AND WOODCARVING, E.J Tangerman. Best book on market; clear, full. If you can cut a potato, you can carve toys, puzzles, chains, etc. Over 464 illustrations. 293pp. 5⅜ × 8½. 20965-2 Pa. $4.95

AMERICAN TRADEMARK DESIGNS, Barbara Baer Capitman. 732 marks, logos and corporate-identity symbols. Categories include entertainment, heavy industry, food and beverage. All black-and-white in standard forms. 160pp. 8⅛ × 11. 23259-X Pa. $6.95

DECORATIVE FRAMES AND BORDERS, edited by Edmund V. Gillon, Jr. Largest collection of borders and frames ever compiled for use of artists and designers. Renaissance, neo-Greek, Art Nouveau, Art Deco, to mention only a few styles. 396 illustrations. 192pp. 8⅜ × 11¼. 22928-9 Pa. $6.00

THE MURDER BOOK OF J.G. REEDER, Edgar Wallace. Eight suspenseful stories by bestselling mystery writer of 20s and 30s. Features the donnish Mr. J.G. Reeder of Public Prosecutor's Office. 128pp. 5⅜ × 8½. (Available in U.S. only)
24374-5 Pa. $3.50

ANNE ORR'S CHARTED DESIGNS, Anne Orr. Best designs by premier needlework designer, all on charts: flowers, borders, birds, children, alphabets, etc. Over 100 charts, 10 in color. Total of 40pp. 8¼ × 11.
23704-4 Pa. $2.50

BASIC CONSTRUCTION TECHNIQUES FOR HOUSES AND SMALL BUILDINGS SIMPLY EXPLAINED, U.S. Bureau of Naval Personnel. Grading, masonry, woodworking, floor and wall framing, roof framing, plastering, tile setting, much more. Over 675 illustrations. 568pp. 6½ × 9¼.
20242-9 Pa. $8.95

MATISSE LINE DRAWINGS AND PRINTS, Henri Matisse. Representative collection of female nudes, faces, still lifes, experimental works, etc., from 1898 to 1948. 50 illustrations. 48pp. 8⅜ × 11¼.
23877-6 Pa. $2.50

HOW TO PLAY THE CHESS OPENINGS, Eugene Znosko-Borovsky. Clear, profound examinations of just what each opening is intended to do and how opponent can counter. Many sample games. 147pp. 5⅜ × 8½.
22795-2 Pa. $2.95

DUPLICATE BRIDGE, Alfred Sheinwold. Clear, thorough, easily followed account: rules, etiquette, scoring, strategy, bidding; Goren's point-count system, Blackwood and Gerber conventions, etc. 158pp. 5⅜ × 8½.
22741-3 Pa. $3.00

SARGENT PORTRAIT DRAWINGS, J.S. Sargent. Collection of 42 portraits reveals technical skill and intuitive eye of noted American portrait painter, John Singer Sargent. 48pp. 8¼ × 11⅛.
24524-1 Pa. $2.95

ENTERTAINING SCIENCE EXPERIMENTS WITH EVERYDAY OBJECTS, Martin Gardner. Over 100 experiments for youngsters. Will amuse, astonish, teach, and entertain. Over 100 illustrations. 127pp. 5⅜ × 8½.
24201-3 Pa. $2.50

TEDDY BEAR PAPER DOLLS IN FULL COLOR: A Family of Four Bears and Their Costumes, Crystal Collins. A family of four Teddy Bear paper dolls and nearly 60 cut-out costumes. Full color, printed one side only. 32pp. 9¼ × 12¼.
24550-0 Pa. $3.50

NEW CALLIGRAPHIC ORNAMENTS AND FLOURISHES, Arthur Baker. Unusual, multi-useable material: arrows, pointing hands, brackets and frames, ovals, swirls, birds, etc. Nearly 700 illustrations. 80pp. 8⅜ × 11¼.
24095-9 Pa. $3.75

DINOSAUR DIORAMAS TO CUT & ASSEMBLE, M. Kalmenoff. Two complete three-dimensional scenes in full color, with 31 cut-out animals and plants. Excellent educational toy for youngsters. Instructions; 2 assembly diagrams. 32pp. 9¼ × 12¼.
24541-1 Pa. $4.50

SILHOUETTES: A PICTORIAL ARCHIVE OF VARIED ILLUSTRATIONS, edited by Carol Belanger Grafton. Over 600 silhouettes from the 18th to 20th centuries. Profiles and full figures of men, women, children, birds, animals, groups and scenes, nature, ships, an alphabet. 144pp. 8⅜ × 11¼.
23781-8 Pa. $4.95

THE BOOK OF WOOD CARVING, Charles Marshall Sayers. Still finest book for beginning student. Fundamentals, technique; gives 34 designs, over 34 projects for panels, bookends, mirrors, etc. 33 photos. 118pp. 7¾ × 10⅝. 23654-4 Pa. $3.95

CARVING COUNTRY CHARACTERS, Bill Higginbotham. Expert advice for beginning, advanced carvers on materials, techniques for creating 18 projects—mirthful panorama of American characters. 105 illustrations. 80pp. 8⅜ × 11. 24135-1 Pa. $2.50

300 ART NOUVEAU DESIGNS AND MOTIFS IN FULL COLOR, C.B. Grafton. 44 full-page plates display swirling lines and muted colors typical of Art Nouveau. Borders, frames, panels, cartouches, dingbats, etc. 48pp. 9⅜ × 12¼. 24354-0 Pa. $6.95

SELF-WORKING CARD TRICKS, Karl Fulves. Editor of *Pallbearer* offers 72 tricks that work automatically through nature of card deck. No sleight of hand needed. Often spectacular. 42 illustrations. 113pp. 5⅜ × 8½. 23334-0 Pa. $3.50

CUT AND ASSEMBLE A WESTERN FRONTIER TOWN, Edmund V. Gillon, Jr. Ten authentic full-color buildings on heavy cardboard stock in H-O scale. Sheriff's Office and Jail, Saloon, Wells Fargo, Opera House, others. 48pp. 9¼ × 12¼. 23736-2 Pa. $3.95

CUT AND ASSEMBLE AN EARLY NEW ENGLAND VILLAGE, Edmund V. Gillon, Jr. Printed in full color on heavy cardboard stock. 12 authentic buildings in H-O scale: Adams home in Quincy, Mass., Oliver Wight house in Sturbridge, smithy, store, church, others. 48pp. 9¼ × 12¼. 23536-X Pa. $4.95

THE TALE OF TWO BAD MICE, Beatrix Potter. Tom Thumb and Hunca Munca squeeze out of their hole and go exploring. 27 full-color Potter illustrations. 59pp. 4¼ × 5½. (Available in U.S. only) 23065-1 Pa. $1.75

CARVING FIGURE CARICATURES IN THE OZARK STYLE, Harold L. Enlow. Instructions and illustrations for ten delightful projects, plus general carving instructions. 22 drawings and 47 photographs altogether. 39pp. 8⅜ × 11. 23151-8 Pa. $2.50

A TREASURY OF FLOWER DESIGNS FOR ARTISTS, EMBROIDERERS AND CRAFTSMEN, Susan Gaber. 100 garden favorites lushly rendered by artist for artists, craftsmen, needleworkers. Many form frames, borders. 80pp. 8¼ × 11. 24096-7 Pa. $3.50

CUT & ASSEMBLE A TOY THEATER/THE NUTCRACKER BALLET, Tom Tierney. Model of a complete, full-color production of Tchaikovsky's classic. 6 backdrops, dozens of characters, familiar dance sequences. 32pp. 9⅜ × 12¼. 24194-7 Pa. $4.50

ANIMALS: 1,419 COPYRIGHT-FREE ILLUSTRATIONS OF MAMMALS, BIRDS, FISH, INSECTS, ETC., edited by Jim Harter. Clear wood engravings present, in extremely lifelike poses, over 1,000 species of animals. 284pp. 9 × 12. 23766-4 Pa. $9.95

MORE HAND SHADOWS, Henry Bursill. For those at their 'finger ends,'' 16 more effects—Shakespeare, a hare, a squirrel, Mr. Punch, and twelve more—each explained by a full-page illustration. Considerable period charm. 30pp. 6½ × 9¼. 21384-6 Pa. $1.95

CHANCERY CURSIVE STROKE BY STROKE, Arthur Baker. Instructions and illustrations for each stroke of each letter (upper and lower case) and numerals. 54 full-page plates. 64pp. 8¼ × 11. 24278-1 Pa. $2.50

THE ENJOYMENT AND USE OF COLOR, Walter Sargent. Color relationships, values, intensities; complementary colors, illumination, similar topics. Color in nature and art. 7 color plates, 29 illustrations. 274pp. 5⅜ × 8½. 20944-X Pa. $4.95

SCULPTURE PRINCIPLES AND PRACTICE, Louis Slobodkin. Step-by-step approach to clay, plaster, metals, stone; classical and modern. 253 drawings, photos. 255pp. 8⅛ × 11. 22960-2 Pa. $7.50

VICTORIAN FASHION PAPER DOLLS FROM HARPER'S BAZAR, 1867-1898, Theodore Menten. Four female dolls with 28 elegant high fashion costumes, printed in full color. 32pp. 9¼ × 12¼. 23453-3 Pa. $3.50

FLOPSY, MOPSY AND COTTONTAIL: A Little Book of Paper Dolls in Full Color, Susan LaBelle. Three dolls and 21 costumes (7 for each doll) show Peter Rabbit's siblings dressed for holidays, gardening, hiking, etc. Charming borders, captions. 48pp. 4¼ × 5½. 24376-1 Pa. $2.25

NATIONAL LEAGUE BASEBALL CARD CLASSICS, Bert Randolph Sugar. 83 big-leaguers from 1909-69 on facsimile cards. Hubbell, Dean, Spahn, Brock plus advertising, info, no duplications. Perforated, detachable. 16pp. 8¼ × 11. 24308-7 Pa. $2.95

THE LOGICAL APPROACH TO CHESS, Dr. Max Euwe, et al. First-rate text of comprehensive strategy, tactics, theory for the amateur. No gambits to memorize, just a clear, logical approach. 224pp. 5⅜ × 8½. 24353-2 Pa. $4.50

MAGICK IN THEORY AND PRACTICE, Aleister Crowley. The summation of the thought and practice of the century's most famous necromancer, long hard to find. Crowley's best book. 436pp. 5⅜ × 8½. (Available in U.S. only) 23295-6 Pa. $6.50

THE HAUNTED HOTEL, Wilkie Collins. Collins' last great tale; doom and destiny in a Venetian palace. Praised by T.S. Eliot. 127pp. 5⅜ × 8½. 24333-8 Pa. $3.00

ART DECO DISPLAY ALPHABETS, Dan X. Solo. Wide variety of bold yet elegant lettering in handsome Art Deco styles. 100 complete fonts, with numerals, punctuation, more. 104pp. 8⅛ × 11. 24372-9 Pa. $4.50

CALLIGRAPHIC ALPHABETS, Arthur Baker. Nearly 150 complete alphabets by outstanding contemporary. Stimulating ideas; useful source for unique effects. 154 plates. 157pp. 8⅜ × 11¼. 21045-6 Pa. $5.95

ARTHUR BAKER'S HISTORIC CALLIGRAPHIC ALPHABETS, Arthur Baker. From monumental capitals of first-century Rome to humanistic cursive of 16th century, 33 alphabets in fresh interpretations. 88 plates. 96pp. 9 × 12. 24054-1 Pa. $4.50

LETTIE LANE PAPER DOLLS, Sheila Young. Genteel turn-of-the-century family very popular then and now. 24 paper dolls. 16 plates in full color. 32pp. 9¼ × 12¼. 24089-4 Pa. $3.50

READY-TO-USE BORDERS, Ted Menten. Both traditional and unusual interchangeable borders in a tremendous array of sizes, shapes, and styles. 32 plates. 64pp. 8¼ × 11. 23782-6 Pa. $3.50

THE WHOLE CRAFT OF SPINNING, Carol Kroll. Preparing fiber, drop spindle, treadle wheel, other fibers, more. Highly creative, yet simple. 43 illustrations. 48pp. 8¼ × 11. 23968-3 Pa. $2.50

HIDDEN PICTURE PUZZLE COLORING BOOK, Anna Pomaska. 31 delightful pictures to color with dozens of objects, people and animals hidden away to find. Captions. Solutions. 48pp. 8¼ × 11. 23909-8 Pa. $2.25

QUILTING WITH STRIPS AND STRINGS, H.W. Rose. Quickest, easiest way to turn left-over fabric into handsome quilt. 46 patchwork quilts; 31 full-size templates. 48pp. 8¼ × 11. 24357-5 Pa. $3.25

NATURAL DYES AND HOME DYEING, Rita J. Adrosko. Over 135 specific recipes from historical sources for cotton, wool, other fabrics. Genuine premodern handicrafts. 12 illustrations. 160pp. 5⅜ × 8½. 22688-3 Pa. $2.95

CARVING REALISTIC BIRDS, H.D. Green. Full-sized patterns, step-by-step instructions for robins, jays, cardinals, finches, etc. 97 illustrations. 80pp. 8¼ × 11. 23484-3 Pa. $3.00

GEOMETRY, RELATIVITY AND THE FOURTH DIMENSION, Rudolf Rucker. Exposition of fourth dimension, concepts of relativity as Flatland characters continue adventures. Popular, easily followed yet accurate, profound. 141 illustrations. 133pp. 5⅜ × 8½. 23400-2 Pa. $3.00

READY-TO-USE SMALL FRAMES AND BORDERS, Carol B. Grafton. Graphic message? Frame it graphically with 373 new frames and borders in many styles: Art Nouveau, Art Deco, Op Art. 64pp. 8¼ × 11. 24375-3 Pa. $3.50

CELTIC ART: THE METHODS OF CONSTRUCTION, George Bain. Simple geometric techniques for making Celtic interlacements, spirals, Kellstype initials, animals, humans, etc. Over 500 illustrations. 160pp. 9 × 12. (Available in U.S. only) 22923-8 Pa. $6.00

THE TALE OF TOM KITTEN, Beatrix Potter. Exciting text and all 27 vivid, full-color illustrations to charming tale of naughty little Tom getting into mischief again. 58pp. 4¼ × 5½. (USO) 24502-0 Pa. $1.75

WOODEN PUZZLE TOYS, Ed Sibbett, Jr. Transfer patterns and instructions for 24 easy-to-do projects: fish, butterflies, cats, acrobats, Humpty Dumpty, 19 others. 48pp. 8¼ × 11. 23713-3 Pa. $2.50

MY FAMILY TREE WORKBOOK, Rosemary A. Chorzempa. Enjoyable, easy-to-use introduction to genealogy designed specially for children. Data pages plus text. Instructive, educational, valuable. 64pp. 8¼ × 11. 24229-3 Pa. $2.50

Prices subject to change without notice.

Available at your book dealer or write for free catalog to Dept. GI, Dover Publications, Inc., 31 East 2nd St. Mineola, N.Y. 11501. Dover publishes more than 175 books each year on science, elementary and advanced mathematics, biology, music, art, literary history, social sciences and other areas.